CW01628833

NEVILLE COOMER

At the Cross - 100 Personal Testimonies of God's Grace in Christ

HAYES
PRESS Christian Publisher

First published by Hayes Press 2019

Copyright © 2019 by Neville Coomer

All rights reserved. No part of this publication may be reproduced, stored or transmitted in any form or by any means, electronic, mechanical, photocopying, recording, scanning, or otherwise without written permission from the publisher. It is illegal to copy this book, post it to a website, or distribute it by any other means without permission.

First edition

This book was professionally typeset on Reedsy.
Find out more at reedsy.com

Contents

DAVID AITKEN (Scotland)

I was 24, I had fallen out with another girlfriend. Then I had an experience on a train, after a day's hill walking, when someone worse for drink threatened me and my friends with a knife. 'What's life all about?' I wondered.

I accepted an offer from a girl at work to go to church, even though I was not interested in religion. The girl was nice. I liked the name of the church. It was simple: "the Church of God." My first experience of church was not great, but I attended a youth group afterwards for discussion. They were asking the question 'who was/is Jesus Christ: man, myth or God? Was he a real person? Is he God?' The leader appeared to have the answer, but I didn't.

After my first visit to church I bought an NIV Bible. Dozens of seemingly intelligent people had translated it from the original languages into English. Previously I had told others that the Bible was rubbish. I had never read any of it for myself. I just formed that impression because I didn't like the behaviour of a few people at that time who seemed to think they were following the Bible. I apologise in advance if you know me and I have had the same effect on you.

I started reading the Bible from the start. My favourite verse is still the same from that time: "In the beginning God created the heavens and the earth." It caused me to start thinking about the world around me and then later about the existence of people. Where did everything come from? The Bible is a difficult book to read. It reflects the world that I live in and does not shy away from the good or the bad. Sometimes God appears harsh and sometimes very forgiving. Questions are big.

Why is there evil? Does God exist? Are the writers truthful? And back to the big question: who is Jesus?

There are a group known as Churches of God and I went to several of them. I enjoyed the company of the Christian people I was beginning to become friendly with, but particularly appreciated some of the older Christian men and women. I admired their lifestyle and their strong, no holding-back faith. I really enjoyed listening to them. It wasn't long after I started reading the Bible that I came across the word 'sin.' I immediately accepted the idea that 'sinner' could easily describe me. I read the 10 Commandments and was surprised that I had broken nine of them. Sin was something I could easily accept. I looked at the world that I lived in and I saw that it was evident everywhere. Perhaps there might be a God who made everything. It was a better explanation for me than everything coming from 'who knows where?'. And the beginning of life? How can life come from no life? A living, everlasting, almighty, all-knowing God who is everywhere could be the source!

I had quite a mixture of friends and colleagues at work (I was an assistant surveyor and purchaser for a small building company) and I spent quite a bit of time finding out other people's views; there was a variety of ideas. Interesting conversations though, and different from the normal day to day stuff. I found it an intriguing thought that only humans appear to be able to even think about whether there is a God. The animal and plant kingdoms don't appear to be interested. Humans are different altogether.

As time went on, I moved towards the 'there is a God' point of view, but my view was not fixed. My biggest stumbling block wasn't whether the Bible was true or not, but the concept of hell. Justice is very important, so it seemed fair to me that God has the right to judge sin. But none of my immediate family were Christians (although my mother's family were very involved with the Salvation Army, I wasn't too sure what that was about) and neither were any of my friends, that I was aware of, apart from my new friends. If hell was real then it was too difficult for me to accept God and the story of Jesus' birth, life, death and resurrection. I understood by then that forgiveness of sin is free. Jesus' death was like a substitution: He died that I might live. He suffered that I might be pardoned and have eternal life. *"All the prophets testify about him* [Jesus] *that everyone who believes in him receives forgiveness of sins through his name"* (Acts 10:43). The thought of hell - if it was real - was like a huge wall that I could not get over (many years later I spent a long time studying the idea and I finally found peace when the wall collapsed). I knew though, that if I was to really trust in God then I could leave everything with Him because it was clear from my reading that He would always do the correct thing and "God is love."

Almost three months after my first visit to church I was still searching, but I still did not have the faith to believe. I decided to attend a Christian summer youth camp just to be of some help. I spent some time on the Monday evening thinking things through again. I cannot remember ever praying before, but I did that night by myself. I said something like: 'God if you are there, save me tomorrow.' In the morning I reluctantly headed off to the prayer meeting in the dining room, not expecting anything to happen. I went in quietly as prayer had already started and the leaders were there with closed eyes. When an older man began to pray, I listened in. He prayed for various things, but what got my attention was his care for others. He then began to pray for a young woman who had meningitis and was seriously unwell. In my head I thought 'it would be nice if someone prayed for me.'

Not knowing that I was in the room, the man then said something like 'and we pray for David that he might be saved.' After this I did not hear much else. Somehow, I had changed (surrendered). I knew from that moment (and in my tears) that I had accepted Christ as my Saviour, and the God of the Bible as my God. God had given me the faith to believe and to trust Him and receive His forgiveness. That was nearly forty years ago, in 1980.

ERIC ARCHIBALD (Scotland)

After attending 100's of gospel meetings, and with the advantage of a godly home, I gradually got the gist of the gospel story; Sunday School input, and not least the hymns and choruses, reinforcing the message. I was given a Bible by my aunt, and turned to it at the age of 9 when alone at home, after a gospel message in which the speaker had urged the necessity of a personal decision to avail myself of God's free gift of eternal life: the consequence of neglecting to do so, and being overtaken by death, being too awful to contemplate. That decision, founded on John 3:16, is the spiritual anchor I continue to depend on.

Bible teaching every evening at home, and the encouragement of a midweek class, brought me to realise that commitment to follow Christ was the best way to show my gratitude for the redeeming work of my Saviour. Friends at the Scottish Camp (run by Churches of God), when I was 12, encouraged me to ask for baptism, which the 2nd chapter of the Acts of the Apostles clearly indicates as the first step in discipleship following conversion. More than 50 years on from being received into fellowship in the Church of God in Glasgow, I am still challenged by the verse in John's gospel ,"Lovest thou Me?" Also, the messages to the churches of God in the book of Revelation are unlike a testimony, in that they are the view of the Lord Himself, and He might have many things to say. Nevertheless, the messages to the churches are like a living testimony in this respect that when they were written, they were not a finished story, and therefore there is room for improvement if only God in His grace has this purpose in granting further time.

KATHLEEN ARCHIBALD (Scotland)

I was brought up in a homely atmosphere, warm with the eternal love of God by parents devoted to His service. I was a simple, uncomplicated child and one day in school, at the age of 7 or 8, I quietly trusted the Lord Jesus as my own Saviour. He must even at that time have been a familiar friend to me, and by the age of 10 I knew His will was that I should be baptised and follow Him as a disciple. This I happily did, and joined many others of the family in the Church of God in Glasgow.

Naturally, at that time I knew little of the Lord's teaching, but over many years I learned to discern His will for my life in the Scriptures, and with the help of the Holy Spirit I have been taught much by the study of His word and by His servants. At the time of my baptism a dear uncle gave me a text from the Bible: *"Trust in the LORD with all your heart, and do not lean on your own understanding. In all your ways acknowledge him, and he will make straight your paths"* (Proverbs 3:5-6).

MARY ARCHIBALD (Scotland)

I was born in 1948 and brought up in Rainford, a Lancashire village situated 5 miles from St. Helens, where the nearest Church of God was situated. I had a happy and stable childhood and attended the Remembrance, Sunday School and gospel meetings of that church. My father, Eric Winstanley, had left the Church of England because he 'never heard the gospel preached.' This realisation came about as he read and studied his Bible. My mother Jane had a similar story and they were married in 1945 in the Church of God in Liverpool. Mum & Dad were very hospitable and I have memories of a Mr Atkinson, an evangelist, and Harry King, whom I called 'Uncle Harry', who often played the mouth organ. Others visited too. Over the years I heard the gospel many, many times, but it really did not have any impact on me.

I started to attend the North West of England Camp in summer, organised by the various churches of God in that district of England, at the age of 9, and to this day I have memories of bell tents, cooking over an open fire, meetings in the big marquee, with speakers including Mr John Drain, Mr George Prasher and Mr Bernard French. The camp was on a very picturesque site overlooking the Ribble Valley with Pendle Hill in the distance.

One night in 1961, the quiet realisation that I was a sinner in need of a Saviour gripped me and I asked Jesus to come into my life. John 3:16 and Romans 10:9 are just two of the verses in the Bible that aided my decision. I was baptised on 1st July, 1961 and added to the Church of God in St. Helens. I helped in the Sunday School in my late teens, and then in 1967 I was transferred to Manchester assembly, where I spent 4 happy years as I did my nursing training at the Royal Infirmary. Friendships formed that continue to this day. In 1971 I was transferred to Edinburgh in Scotland where I did my midwifery training.

In 1973 I married Eric and moved to Glasgow. Here we raised our 5 children. For a number of years I have been coping with cancer. The experience has strengthened my faith and I know God gives me His grace for each day, and this faith can be a powerful witness to others. What the future holds is in God's hands.

FREDERICK ARTHUR BANKS (England)

He was born in Ipswich, Suffolk of humble parentage and at an early age suffered from the great drawback of continuous ill-health, having a disposition to what was then known as 'consumption', a disease from which he eventually died. His father and mother were believers in the Lord Jesus. Both died when he was a boy. The story, in his own words, was:

'I well remember the dying moments of my dear mother. She called me to her side and, with fervent appeal, besought me to meet her in heaven. Clasping her hands firmly I promised her I would. Soon after, she passed away to be with her Lord. My grief was great. Alas, the memory of that scene was soon effaced, and I still went on unsaved – 'Careless of my soul immortal, heeding not the call of God.' The prayers of my mother did not go unanswered. A year or two later I was aroused to see my lost and utterly ruined condition as a sinner, and that it was only by faith in the Lord Jesus Christ, and His finished work on Calvary, I could be saved. I believed in Him, and the cleansing power of His precious blood, and rejoiced in the knowledge of sins forgiven.'

Not long after his conversion, his father's state of health declined rapidly. Just before his death, he rejoiced that Fred would one day reunite with his mother and him in heaven. Later, Fred made great progress in God's service, even as a young man. Though his bodily strength was weak, he gave himself fully to the Lord's work as an evangelist and teacher, travelling not only throughout Great Britain and Ireland, but in the far-away West Indian Islands, where many were led to the Lord through his preaching. His short but full life ended in

Devonshire.

After his death, articles he had written were brought together and printed by The Needed Truth Publishing Office in November 1898 under the title 'Spiritual Growth and Other Writings.' He also wrote many gospel tracts. It was said of him that he was no ordinary pioneer in the things of God. The truth of the church and churches of God, with kindred truths, had been neglected for generations. He sought to recover and teach clearly the principles of churches of God – God's spiritual house as distinct from the truth of the church which is Christ's body. His physical weakness and frailty did not have the effect of making him timid and nervous. 'In the things of God he was lion-hearted and his spirit rose superior to his weakness.'

EMMANUEL BASSEY (Nigeria)

My mother encouraged me to attend Qua Iboe Church Sunday School as a boy. I became used to going to church meetings with my parents. I attended the church catechism class for a year before being interviewed, baptised and received into the church at a young age.

In 1963 I left my home town of Idua-Eket to live in Lagos with my eldest brother Udo. He had no interest in church. I was able to attend the Assemblies of God Mission because it was near where I lived. Nearing the end of 1963 I came across a gospel campaign by the Church of God in Surulere. We received an invitation leaflet identifying the venue and advertising the speaker as Mr George Prasher, B.Sc. (Manchester). There were week-long meetings starting at 7:00 p.m. Udo was most surprised that a graduate with a Bachelor of Science degree could be an evangelist. He wanted to meet the gentleman. The message of salvation was preached and the work of the Holy Spirit in his heart brought Udo under conviction of sin. He got saved and then soon after was baptised as a disciple of Christ and added to the Church of God in Surulere before the end of the year.

Udo's lifestyle changed remarkably. He was in debt, however, before his conversion. Early in 1964 he faced a great temptation to take a bribe at work, but he refused. He was employed by the Federal Civil Service in the Ministry of Finance, the department responsible then for the issue of import licences. I could not see why he refused to accept the money offered which could solve his financial difficulty. The expatriate Managing Director of the company that offered the bribe was so impressed in the way Udo acted because of his faith that he offered him the job of Personal Assistant Director in the very company in Lagos who offered the bribe illegally! Udo stepped into the limelight of enviable social status amid the financial boom in the country in 1964.

Udo's conversion and stand taken for Christ's sake had a great impact on me. He invited me to come to the Sunday School in the Church of God in Surulere. Samuel Brown, one of the teachers, taught me to pay heed to what the Bible said. Romans 10:1-13 helped me to see how I could be saved and have the assurance of salvation. I remember praying at my bedside, owning up to my sins and guilt, and thanking God that Jesus died to save me. That was in Easter time 1964. It was so real to me. In August that year I was baptised and added to the Church of God. In September, when I resumed school, I had so much joy witnessing to fellow-students. The Gideon Pocket Bible I carried everywhere. 'Uncle' Willie Stewart, an evangelist, encouraged me to use gospel leaflets in testifying of Christ. Brown Okeke was the first student convinced by my testimony and gave his life to Christ. He, too, was baptised and added and is now in the Church of God in Port Harcourt.

In 1967 'Mum & Dad' Prasher chose me to live with them in the UK as one of the postscripts of their work in Nigeria. God used them in the furtherance of my education and exposure to know God's will for my life. Seven wonderful years of unbroken stay in the UK passed quickly. I returned to Nigeria in 1973 after graduating in Electrical and Electronic Engineering. I worked for ICL, Nigeria Ltd. as a computer engineer for 4 years and for SCPA Nigeria PLC as a sales engineer first, then a service engineer for 16 years. From 1992 I was self-employed under Hambia Nigeria Ltd., which specialised in maintenance and repairs of commercial generators. By 2002 I found it impracticable to combine secular employment with my role in Radio Evangelism. My wife and I prayed and waited on the Lord for the way to go. The Lord's word guided us, *"Anyone who puts a hand to the plough and then looks back is not fit for the kingdom of God"* (Luke 9:62).

I became involved in Search for Truth Gospel broadcasting weekly from ELWA Station in Monrovia, Liberia from 1984 – 1988. Later I was with Radio Station OYO in Ibadan, Oyo State from 1997 – 2001. I was responsible for the main messages in English. Then I moved on to the FM Radio Station in Port Harcourt, Rivers State, from 2002 – 2005. I thank God for enabling me to 'tell the old, old story of Jesus and His love' to many friends, some of whom I may never meet in this life. I still joy in gospel witness and leading souls to Christ.

PEGGY BENNISON (England)

From my earliest years I was brought up to know about the Lord Jesus, but it was not until the Haringey Crusade that I committed my life to Christ. In 1954 Billy Graham came to England to preach Christ. There had been a great deal of prayer and preparation for this visit and the Lord certainly answered those prayers. I was working in London then and we had a very keen Christian young lady who took a group of us to Haringey. The arena was packed. The choir and audience sang hymns, then Billy Graham gave his message. The only thing I remember of this was the Bible text: *"All our righteousnesses are as filthy rags"* (Isaiah 64:6). Mr Graham invited people to make a decision to accept Christ into their lives. Quietly a number of folk moved to the front. He then said 'I know there are more ready to accept Christ.' I knew then that I must take a stand and went forward. This was the most important decision of my whole life. My younger sister also accepted the Saviour. Soon afterwards my elder sister died and I found God is a God of comfort. At cookery classes I met a girl who belonged to the Baptist Church and I started to go along there where I was baptised. My father began to teach me about the Churches of God and I became a member of the Church of God in Wembley. I have found the Lord Jesus to be a wonderful friend. He has won my heart and has been the greatest help in good and bad times. I can say in all sincerity, 'All this and heaven too.'

MARY BOLT (England)

I was born in Atherton, Lancashire on 28 February, 1942. My sister Ruth was born a year later and my brother Peter in 1944. Dad was a shot-firer in the coal mine and worked at Chanter's Colliery in Tyldesley. In 1945 he was involved in an accident underground. He managed to get all his men to safety, but when he tried to jump into the tub (coal carrier) he was trapped over the side of it. The roof above, where he was, caved in. His back was broken and he was in hospital for 18 months, paralysed; then, sadly he passed away.

When I was 14 I got saved. I don't know what led me to this, except sitting at the dining table with a piece of paper and pencil, and I wrote: 'Mummy, I am saved.' I remember leaving it for Mum to find, then going out to play, but no memories after that. When I was 8 I was baptised. That was on September 3rd, 1950 in Leigh assembly hall.

I passed the 11 plus and went to Leigh Girls' Grammar School in Windermere Road. I was there for 6 years then got a job in the Art Room in the Catalogue Production department of a Manchester Mail Order company. Three years were spent there and then I trained as a GPO Telephonist. At 19 years of age I met Martin Bolt from Birkenhead and we married on 14th September, 1963. We have a son, Christopher and a daughter Nicola. They are both saved by God's grace, as are our children-in-law, Tracey & John, for which I am eternally grateful.

For a while, when the children were growing up , I began to doubt my salvation as I had no blinding light experience of it. It worried me for a long time and I lost hours of sleep over it. The problem was, had I simply accepted the gospel message because I was brought up in a

Christian home, or had I really believed Jesus had died for my personal sins? I kept this to myself for many years. I got the assurance and was more at peace with myself. One day, after the Remembrance at our church, I was talking to Doreen Seddon and mentioned how I had felt about my salvation. She was so kind and understanding and since that conversation I have never doubted it.

I have now been in 'The Fellowship' / Churches of God for 55 years at the time I am writing this and thank the Lord daily for it, and for my friends in Birkenhead and other assemblies of churches of God. I also thank Him daily for my wonderful husband and family and also for the following generations, all being well, that they might know Christ as their Saviour too.

PHYLLIS BOLT (England)

I am very thankful that I was brought up in a Christian home. My father used to read the Scriptures to us each day, and explain them. He also used to sing choruses, never missing an opportunity to speak of his Saviour to friends, workmates, and acquaintances. Being of a very timid nature, while at Junior School I remember reading the 27th Psalm while waiting for the Scripture lesson to start. It was a great help to me; *"the Lord is my light and my salvation, of whom then shall I be afraid?"* Although I had grown up to love the Lord Jesus and to trust in Him knowing He had died for me, at the age of 13 I really wanted to be baptised. Not having a verse to prove I was truly saved, I realised I must do something about it. Then my father read Isaiah 53:5, *"But He was wounded for our* [i.e. mine, too] *transgressions, He was bruised for our* [my] *iniquities: the chastisement of our* [my] *peace was upon Him; and with His stripes we are* [I am] *healed."* I claimed this verse for my own then was baptised. Although I have tried to be obedient, I feel I have done very little in return for all Christ has done for me. Malcolm Horne once gave us a text with a calendar for Christmas and New Year, which said, *"Let us go boldly before the throne of grace, that we may find grace to help us in times of need."*

'Great God, and dost Thou condescend
To be my Father and my Friend?
I, a poor child, and Thou so high,
The Lord of earth and sea and sky!'
(Ann Taylor)

JIM BRINDLE (Scotland)

At primary school we were taught good writing, good arithmetic, and good grammar. Although it was never taught these could earn you a place in heaven, somehow you could by good behaviour and being a 'good' person. This was odd to me. For one thing, the language in the playground was often very poor. Between the bigger boys squabbles and fights took place, some quite violent.

At home things were very different. The Bible was read every morning and unfailingly at the end of the day. As a result of this, though still young in years, I knew what sin was; how it can destroy peoples' lives the world over, and that Satan could ruin my life too. So, in my heart I longed that Jesus, the sinner's Saviour, would draw near to me and impart peace and give me eternal life. This longing was at last realised in the late afternoon of 7th August, 1950. I no longer resisted God's love and His way of salvation. I repented of my sins, put all my trust in Jesus my Saviour, and was released from condemnation. This gave me indescribable peace and joy.

'I looked to Jesus there on high,
From death upraised to glory.
I trusted in His power to save,
Believed the old, old story.'
(Daniel W. Whittle)

COLIN BROOKS (Scotland)

It began, I suppose, around 70-odd years ago when I was born into a family of God-fearing and hard-working folks. One might wish that my story could be painted in the vibrant colours of a 'Damascus Road' experience, but not so. In telling it all, I am conscious of the ordinariness of my experiences and yet when one can tell of a personal encounter with the Saviour and a lifelong commitment thereafter, there is surely nothing ordinary about this! If I cannot claim deliverance from some of the grosser sins that others might have known, I was never in any doubt that I was nevertheless a sinner, 'By nature and practice and all, utterly lost and ruined by the fall!' as the old hymn puts it.

However, I was twice blessed, having been born into a godly family and thus shielded from much of the world's less desirable influences. Not just that, but I was so privileged to have a mother who truly loved the Lord and although not spared to us for long, for she passed away when I was only 9 years of age and my younger brother going on for 7. Yet among the memories of her that I treasure one lingers, and that is of her sitting with two of us at the family table, one on her knee, telling us of a Saviour who loved us and died on the cross for our salvation. In these early years, brief as they were, there was laid a good foundation. So it was, like Timothy of old in the Bible story, I was blessed with a godly mother and grandmother too who taught me something of the *"sacred writings"* (2 Timothy 3:15) which can make us wise unto salvation.

Now someone might well ask, 'But when did you become a believer on the Lord Jesus Christ?' My answer simply is this: 'I do not recall a time when I did not believe!' However, I can say that a very short time after my mother's passing, I was sitting in a little gospel hall in the mining village of Ashgill, Lanarkshire, on a Sunday evening listening to a message from that well-known text in John 3:16. The speaker was not particularly eloquent as I recall, but I believe God used that dear man to arrest my wandering thoughts so that I found myself challenged by this question: 'Do I truly believe that God loves me and gave His only Son for me?' The answer was a positive 'Yes!' and therein was I given by the Spirit of God the assurance of being a possessor of eternal life, the promise of God to all who believe in Jesus.

Having lost our mother, my father took on the task of being both father and mother to 2 boys at a time of great personal hardship and difficulty in his life. It is to his credit he carried on the good work which had begun in earlier years. Shortly afterwards, I was baptised and added to the Church of God in Ashgill. Years have rolled on and many times I must have disappointed the Lord, but with the hymnwriter I can truly say, 'He (Jesus) is not a disappointment to me!' So, as I ponder God's dealings with me I know I am and always will be eternally grateful for all the influences for good which in God's own way were used to bring me to saving faith in the Lord Jesus Christ.

ALEX BROWN (Scotland)

"For me alone." These words are taken from a hymn where the first verse reads:

"Was it for me, for me alone,
The Saviour left His glorious throne;
The dazzling splendours of the sky,
Was it for me He came to die?"
(John M. Whyte)

The words certainly apply to my conversion story. The story is simple and began a long time ago, just after the Second World War . Many commodities were scarce and rationing was still in existence. One thing hard to get was paper. We could nearly be buried in it today, but then it was expensive and not wasted.

At the end of the 1940s we had arranged for a Christian evangelist called Geoff Mutimer to visit our church in Wishaw and hold meetings. Some were for children. To illustrate a point in his message, he made the children cut out a paper cross. The paper used was from a shorthand notebook through a friend of the family. This cross I kept and managed to cut out 2 more. They were precious keepsakes from a man who told simply and clearly the story of Jesus' crucifixion. Many aspects of the message remain imprinted on my mind to this day. In these times, housewives retained all sorts of little boxes containing dressmaking and other items. It just seemed right to me to take one of these little round boxes full of plain pins and pin the paper crosses to the carpet in our living-room floor.

Early one Sunday morning before setting off for our church service, I was 'pinning away' and pricked my finger. I spoke to my Mum about it while she was making the bed nearby. I had heard of the cruel nails that were driven through Jesus' hands and feet. A pinprick, a droplet of blood and the pain of it, caused me to think! I asked Mum if Jesus really suffered these things. She confirmed this to be true. My young mind reasoned that if a pinprick was so sore, what must have the jagged nails been like! Did He really love me so much to suffer all this for me. Then there was the crown of thorns, the scourged back, and the bleeding cheeks. Did he really suffer all those things too for me?

What could a Christian mother reply but, 'Yes, it was true.' That focused my mind. So, as a young boy of 8 I realised that 'It was for me.' He came from heaven to die and pay the price God required to take away my sin. Later, I learned and appreciated the very real and true words of Paul the apostle of the Lord Jesus, *"The Son of God who loved me, and gave Himself up for me"* (Galatians 2:20).

I have learned a lot more since, but it still causes tears to come to my eyes when I think of the chorus of the hymn, giving answer to the first verse:

"It was for me, yes, all for me,
O love of God, so great, so free!
O wondrous love, I'll shout and sing,
He died for me, my Lord and King!"

JOAN BROWN (England)

During the Second World War, while the German Air Force was bombing Liverpool, I was born under the stairs in my parents' home in St Helens, Lancashire, England, in September 1940.

For the first ten years of my life I was brought up in our Christian family along with my two older brothers, John and Gordon, who I knew were saved and had been baptised. So, at the age of 10, I asked the Lord Jesus to come into my heart and life. I did this as I knelt beside my little bed in the front bedroom upstairs. The date was 19th March, 1951, which was my mother's birthday, but regrettably I never told anyone what I had done. This would have been great news for all my family. Maybe it was because I had always believed that Jesus had died for me, but by asking Him into my heart I thought I would feel like a different little person - which I didn't, so I hesitated telling anyone .

So my simple story is that I was born under the stairs and was 'born again' up the stairs in the house where I lived for 25 years before getting married to my dear husband Alex in 1966. Together we have both continued on the disciple pathway in Wishaw Assembly for the past 53 years, knowing the Lord's blessing for which we are both truly thankful.

LYNNE BUTLER (England)

It was the middle of August 1977 when I met my Saviour, Jesus Christ. I was walking to my Mum & Dad's house up Sowerby New Road. I had to walk through Sowerby Bridge, which meant going past Christ Church at the bottom of Tuel Lane. It was cold so I was rushing, but something made me slow down and look at a poster on the fence that made me think twice. It said, "Need a change of life? Why not pop in for a service?" I thought 'Yes, I do; yes, I will!' So when arriving at the house I told Mum about how I felt. I said "I think God has called for me." She answered, "Well, good for you. Look in the phone book for your nearest Methodist Church – your Dad and I were both brought up Methodist."

I found the church, St. Paul's, and the last Sunday in August was the first service I went to. I was very nervous but everybody made me welcome, explained anything I couldn't understand, and so on. In May 1998 I spoke to a lady about my faith but felt I should be giving or doing more. She then asked if I had been christened. "No" was my response. "Well, what more can you do or give?" was her reply. So, I was christened in 1998 and made a member of the church.

However, since then, I met and fell in love with Robert Butler, now my husband. After we married I went along with him to Waterloo Hall, the meeting place of the Church of God in Halifax. I must admit I found it all a bit hard to understand for a while. We had spoken about baptism and what it meant in the Bible, but I always said a most definite "No" to it as I had already been christened. Then after a time Bob, my father-in-law, was speaking at one of the services and talking about water and what it was used for, you know, washing and drinking and, you've guessed it, baptism. All of a sudden, I got very excited and knew that was what was right to do as a believer in the Lord Jesus, and I had to do it. God had spoken to me through him and I know I was now doing what the Lord Jesus had wanted.

ROBERT JOHN BUTLER (England)

At home, with some of my more important papers, I keep 2 special photos of myself as a child. The first was taken around my first birthday; the second shows me, still with a cheeky smile, several years later. Obviously I have no recollections of babyhood, but I can just about remember the second being taken. Sometime between these two captured moments in my early life I had a playmate called Percy. He was my friend. Percy was our cat and at my persistent teasing he would go off and hide, which made the game more fun. One day though, he got his own back. With one swipe of his paw he gave me a neat scratch on my left cheek, which I know is true, having heard the story from my parents, plus the fact I have a scar on my face for life!

Brought up in a Christian home, my parents also told me about Jesus and I believed on Him from an early age. 'So how can you prove you're a real Christian?' you might well ask, particularly as I can't remember exactly when I took Him as my Saviour. Well, in answering this question, I can say most definitely I have real peace in my heart and this peace is based on my faith in Jesus Christ who died on the cross for me. God's word says, *"Being therefore justified by faith, we have peace with God through our Lord Jesus Christ"* (Romans 5:1). My peace with God is His gift and unlike the scar on my face, it's not just for life, but is mine for all eternity. Do you have this peace too?

Along with Christian friends I can now sing with real meaning, to the God and Father of my Saviour and Lord, the verse of the hymn:

"No more the heirs of wrath,
The smile of peace we see,
And triumphing o'er sin and death
We praise and worship Thee."
(Augustus Toplady)

MARY CASE (Scotland)

I will never forget Christmas Day, 1955. I was 13 and regularly attended the Sunday School of the Church of God in Methil, Fife, in Scotland. Two friends of my own age also attended and the three of us were invited by a lady called Catherine Montgomery to have lunch with her family, and also go to the gospel meeting in the evening. After the gospel meeting ended, Catherine asked us if we wanted to be 'saved', by each one of us making the decision to believe on the Lord Jesus as our personal Saviour. Not fully understanding what she meant, I said 'Yes.' My friends said they couldn't stay any longer and had to go home.

A Mr Montgomery and a Mr Paton, who were in the church, spoke to me and we read together a few well-known Bible verses, with John 3:16 being the one most referred to. I remember the earnestness of those two men as they spoke about salvation and although I had no sudden revelation of the scriptures at that time, I knew for sure that very night that Jesus had died on the cross for me, and from then on I sought to grow in the knowledge of Him as my Saviour and Lord.

NENG DO CIN (Myanmar)

I was born in 1948. I was 15 years of age when I heard Go Khua Hau preaching from Hebrews 2:3, *"How shall we escape if we ignore such great salvation?"* That touched my heart. I believed and was born again. I was baptised in 1963 and when the Church of God in Suangphei was planted in 1966, I gave myself to join it. Now the Lord has entrusted to me the responsibility of 'shepherding the sheep' (people in the church) in Suangphei, for which I give thanks to God.

JOCELYN COOMER (Scotland)

When I was 7, it was my Mum who told me, when I asked her about 'being saved', that I should pray to God, say sorry for all my sins, ask for forgiveness, and thank God for sending His Son into this world. This I did.

This one genuine decision I sincerely believe is enough to give me a passport into heaven. In John 10:28–29 Jesus says, *"I give them eternal life, and they will never perish, and no one will snatch them out of my hand. My Father, who has given them to me, is greater than all, and no one is able to snatch them out of the Father's hand. I and the Father are one."* However, over my childhood years, for my own assurance, I would often tell God that I really did believe in Jesus and thank Him over and over again for sending His Son to die for my sins.

Now as an adult, most nights, especially in the winter, as I am praying for the homeless and thanking God for a roof over my head and a warm bed to sleep in, I thank God for allowing me the honour of having an eternal home with Him in heaven.

NEVILLE COOMER (England)

My grandfather was a gold prospector who struck gold when he went to Australia. He never worked again. He had a white cottage in Hampshire with some acres, a Jersey cow, a large orchard, and a big conservatory with a fruitful vine. Inside this hothouse he sat on a deckchair and taught me how to tell the time with his pocket watch and chain. He also taught me to value time.

My father was a poultry farmer, breeding turkeys and chickens, guinea fowl, egg-collecting, haymaking and had a donkey for pulling a cart. He also kept bees and sold honey. He taught me the value of work. I think he thought it was good for the physique, good for the mind, and good for the soul, and could keep you out of mischief. My mother got me to join the church choir – until my voice broke, then I pumped the organ, rather than go into the congregation with her - and I got paid for it!

Towards the end of the 1939–45 war, Colin, my brother, and I were coming home from school when a German plane shot at us. It missed; but a bullet was found later in our conservatory! When I was 16 years old, I survived a very near drowning accident several miles from home. We had been boating and swimming and I suddenly got cramp. Fortunately, they pushed me to the bank and 'did the necessary.' I was at this time still not a believer in the Lord Jesus, nor did I show any interest. At 18 years of age I was called up for National Service and went into the army's medical corps. Here I quickly learnt about drill and how to swear like a trooper! I was sent to Hamburg in Germany and there I saw the devastation of war; the results of bombing on cities

– no buildings standing and old people gathering scraps out of garbage bins. The effects of war were horrible.

One day I decided to go to a 'Garrison Church' in Altona. As the Germans came out of the building we went in. We were worshipping God in the same church, yet as soldiers we were fighting each other. Was the world mad? Nothing made sense. I was curious but found no answers. A few months later I was demobbed, came home, and went to Sparsholt for agricultural training. I left my army uniform behind but still swore like a trooper. My brother Colin said to me, 'Can't you say a sentence without swearing?' My Germany experience left me with unanswered questions. Then I met a girl at the Farm Institute and she told me about some gospel meetings near my home. I cycled 7 miles each way in going to hear the message. It was all too clear. I was a sinner (Romans 3:23) and needed to be saved. Unforgiven sinners would be punished. I could have salvation for free (Romans 6:23). The free gift of God is eternal life in Christ Jesus our Lord. I could not save myself, only God's Son, Jesus Christ, could save me. I had to believe that He died for my sins, and when I did believe, all my sins would be forgiven (Acts 16:30–31). Then I would become a child of God and have eternal life (John 1:12).

As soon as I went to that gospel hall I recognised some former school friends and that proved helpful. I returned to the hall some 7 times. I knew beyond doubt I was a sinner and needed to be saved. I returned home one night as a believer. I was saved and happy. I was 21 years old at this time. I remember we sang a hymn that included a line, "He can e'en the vilest save." Eventually I told my father. He said, 'Yes, I know and I saw a change in you, but we'll see how long it lasts'. A miracle happened. My swearing immediately stopped without any effort on my part. Many years later, before my father died, I said to him, 'Dad, do you remember what you said, "We'll see how long it lasts."' 'Me, I never said that.' 'You did,' I replied, 'but it has lasted and I still believe.'

From Sparsholt I went to Harper Adams College, newly saved, and here I was tested as to my new-found beliefs. I visited friends, read my Bible, and asked a lot of questions. Then I went to Reading University and on to Stoke Mandeville, where I was 'Experimental Co-ordinator.' Here I met the Resident Vet, Helen Archibald. Baptism was my next hurdle. I had been christened in the Church of England. The people I knew practised Household Baptism. I had learned that the Bible taught salvation first, followed by water baptism by immersion (Acts 2:41-42). I was baptised and added to the Church of God in Glasgow. In due course I married Helen. Our three children are all saved and baptised. We have 6 grandchildren, and several are saved eternally through accepting Jesus as their personal Saviour.

JIM CRANSON (Scotland)

My attitude towards God changed as a result of much heart-searching by myself, and many prayers by others. I was raised in a happy working-class home and as an only child my parents saw to it that I lacked for nothing that was humanly possible to make or purchase. As my childhood requirements were just after the Second World War, the making and purchasing of toys etc. was not the easiest of tasks.

Both my parents were associated with the Salvation Army, so I knew from an early age what it was like to be taken to a religious service. My lasting memory was of the choir of songsters singing and the band playing; both performed with great vigour and feeling. Whilst I was still comparatively young my parents ceased to be active members of the Salvation Army, with the result that after a time I began to attend a Sunday School which was very near my home. The format of this Sunday School was very different to what I had been accustomed to, nevertheless it was no less sincere. Bible stories were faithfully told every Sunday afternoon by men and women who obviously had great feeling and love for God's word, so much so that by the time I had reached my early teens the necessity of having a personal belief in God and His Son, Jesus Christ, was clearly brought home to me. It was gently pointed out that it simply was not enough to attend religious services, but absolutely necessary to believe on the central character of the Bible, and that was the Son of God and what He did for me and others.

By the age of 20/21 I had started attending the church's evening service, which was called a gospel meeting. It was at these events I came to understand not only did God love the world, i.e. everyone, but He loved me as an individual; and even though I had been disobedient to Him by not obeying His word, He had shown His care and affection by opening up the way whereby I would be given the opportunity to change my ways and become obedient to Him. After one such gospel meeting, the preacher asked me if I had made God's Son my own personal Saviour. When I hesitated, he opened up his Bible at John 3:16 whereupon he began to read the verse. After he had finished, he asked me to read and place my own name in it and went on to explain how this was done. When I came to the words 'world' and 'whoever', I was to insert my own name to emphasise the fact that God gave His Son for me so that I would never perish but have everlasting life. I was saved that night and have rejoiced ever since in the knowledge that God's Son Jesus Christ is now and always will be my personal Saviour.

I found out some time afterwards that a number of Christians had been praying to God that I would make the right decision. Truly, 'God moves in a mysterious way, His wonders to perform.'

ROY DICKSON (Scotland)

At 7 or 8 years of age I can remember ordering my father and brother to stand outside my room while I prayed to God. My grandfather was a Mission Hall preacher among shipyard works in the West of Scotland and my great uncle, who wrote "All the Days of my Life" was a missionary in the Nigerian bush during the Biafran war. Father was an elder in the Church of Scotland and a believer in the Lord Jesus as his personal Saviour. I went to church but never heard the gospel preached there. It was not until my early twenties that I had the assurance of salvation.

I must go back to my teens, however. At 16, I had a growing awareness that Jesus is the Son of God, but I cannot recall what made me think in that way. I guess that reading my Bible brought a general feeling of deficiency. In fact, I remember thinking I must give my life to Jesus Christ, but at that time, I thought this meant becoming a missionary. That was probably due to the influence of my family, though they did not suggest it. I remember answering a question at school which asked, 'What is the most important thing in your life?' with the words, 'Trying to live as we were shown 2,000 years ago.' I was not sure if I was saved; certainly I had no assurance of it. I left High School and went to University. With no prayer life and living away from home I was an easy prey to any so-called religious teaching, not really knowing my Bible. In November 1975 I met up with the Moonies and was so caught up with the cult that despite being only a short time away from graduation, I decided to give up my studies to become a Moonie missionary. My professors were concerned and my parents were distressed by my decision.

Oh, yes! I had begun praying to Sun Myung Moon, who is regarded by the cult as a second Christ. I prayed intensely that I would be shown the true way of life by a certain date and I fasted that the answer might come. To become a full-time Moonie missionary was my understanding of the answer. It cost me a lot to make that decision. What then? By the mercy of God, through the distress of my family, whom I loved dearly, I was persuaded to abandon my intentions for the time being and I stayed on at University to get my degree, much to the relief of my professors. I must add, however, that I was still in sympathy with Moon and what he taught.

In 1976 I spent some time in France. Having little money and feeling lonely, I began reading parts of the Bible I hadn't read before, such as Romans, and other 'epistles.' I also began praying to God to show me whether Jesus or Moon was the true Christ. I was still confused and uncertain about spiritual matters, so after completing my studies I applied for a job in Merseyside. I was disappointed at not getting it and decided to take a single year's course at a Technical College.

I was spiritually confused and generally disillusioned and drifting. I shall never forget standing in the college enrolment queue in such a condition, when immediately standing behind me was a disciple of Jesus Christ. God had led us both to join the same year of the same course on the same day at the same place and at the same time. God's ways are past tracing out. It's a long story, but within a week I was attending gospel meetings and having discussions about Christ. I remember praying in tears that God might show me who really was the Christ – Jesus or Moon. This was my biggest predicament. One thing that deeply impressed me was the thought that the reference to Jesus as the 'Lamb of God' was not so much a reference to His gentleness as to His sacrificial death on the cross. This was a big pointer to me and began to strike at the Moonie heresy. By Christmas 1977 I was sure at last that Jesus is the Christ and told my father this, much to his relief. Through sustained discussion there was a gradual process of throwing out the evil of Moon's teachings in the light of the Word of God, until at last I found the assurance of eternal life.

By the time I had finished with college, I had learned about believers' baptism. I questioned why I could not be baptised in a Church of Scotland. The minister said he preferred it, but could not carry it out as it would offend the congregation. I was offered a job in Berkshire and joined a little group of evangelical Christians. After a year I was baptised with them, but became unsettled as a result of their disunity. God's truth was leading me to His house, His dwelling place on earth. Some of the friends I had left behind in Scotland wrote to me occasionally. One in particular contacted a friend of his in Surrey, who, in turn, invited me to his home and, subsequently, to a church of God. My real interest in divine truth revived. I quickly saw God's pattern of collective testimony and service from Acts 2:41-42 and elsewhere, and was added to the Lord.

As I read my Bible I am continually amazed as the truths that unfold themselves show me the greatness of God's house into which, by His grace, I've been brought. It's wonderful how things, of which I had no conception when I first came into 'The Fellowship' have now become clear. I thought at first I knew most of what was involved, but I guess I knew very little. I'm saddened when people who have learned these things appear not to appreciate them.

I'm always wary of appearing to advise others, but from my own experience I'd say to young folk in particular to get to know the Scriptures in their youth. If I had done that, I could easily have destroyed some of the theories and arguments of subtle men that almost ruined my life. One thing more: I believe it is important to try hard to be in the right condition of heart to know the Lord's guidance. We can then leave it to Him and we shall recognise His guidance in retrospect.

TERRY DOUGAN (Northern Ireland)

A testimony is a solemn declaration of facts often given under oath in a court of law. This testimony relates to the story of my salvation which took place in 1950, almost seventy years ago.

Mr Arthur Jones, an evangelist from South Wales, was visiting Belfast that year to conduct a series of Gospel meetings in Shiloh Hall, the meeting place of the Church of God. It was customary to have an open air meeting in the city centre at Cornmarket after the evening service. In the course of his address to those around and passers-by, he appealed to his hearers to be ready for the imminent return of the Lord Jesus Christ from heaven. This is a wonderful event which the scriptures tell us about in several places, especially in 1 Thessalonians 4. It is here that it is spelled out as to how this will happen. It is quite dramatic and worth serious consideration. Mr Jones emphasised the need to be ready for this event as and when it occurs. The absolute certainty of it occurring was stressed on more than one occasion. This is the time when the Lord will come and receive all those who have trusted Him as Saviour. They will be caught up to heaven to be with Him for eternity. Those who have not believed on Him would be left behind. This was what alarmed my younger sister, Nora, as she wanted to be ready should it happen any time soon.

Immediately after the open air meeting was finished, my mother invited Mr Jones for supper, along with some other friends. They travelled by car to our home where Nora had a conversation with Mr Jones which resulted in her accepting the Lord Jesus as her Saviour. My father and I arrived somewhat later and the door was opened by my sister who greeted my father with the words 'Daddy, I'm saved.' That completely shook me to the core. This 'revelation' meant that should the Lord return that night I would not be ready to meet Him and would be left behind. Yes, a scary thought with eternal consequences. My parents and my sister would be caught up to meet the Lord. I would be left. I can tell you, I did not eat much supper as the significance of this came home to me.

I left the room and went into the kitchen looking somewhat downcast; my mother asked what was wrong. I explained the effect of my sister's declaration earlier and the realisation that I was as yet unsaved and therefore not ready for Christ's return. This would result in my eternal banishment from heaven. Mother reminded me of one of my favourite Bible stories, concerning the apostle Paul in the jail in Philippi. Paul and his friend Silas had been beaten and put in the jail. Despite this treatment they sang hymns and prayed to God.

Suddenly there was an earthquake; the prison was shaken; the prisoners' bonds were broken and the doors were opened. When the jailor saw this he was about to commit suicide but Paul told him to do himself no harm as all the prisoners were still there. The jailor leapt into the prison and asked, "*Sirs, what must I do to be saved?*" Paul replied, *"Believe on the Lord Jesus and you shall be saved."* The man believed and was saved. I too believed this message and I was saved too for eternity. Should the Lord return I was and am ready to meet Him.

A few years later I was baptised and added to the assembly in Belfast where, by the grace of God, I have in the words of Acts 2 *"continued steadfastly in the apostles' teaching."*

DAVID ELSON (England)

I was the second of 6 children. My grandfather played cricket and captained the school team. There was no doubting his leadership qualities. He was a strict disciplinarian both in his own home and in the church. Those of his own family who did not follow closely in his footsteps, tended to be ostracised, at least for a time. My father, with something of his mother in him and with the gracious influence of his wife, my mother, steered a more relaxed approach to family life, for which I am forever grateful.

From toddling days I attended Sunday School, took my place 'behind' at the Remembrance Service as I was not in the church, and went to gospel meetings every week. About the age of 7/8, two men moved to Birmingham and both of them took a spiritual interest in me. Howard Darke became my Sunday School teacher, Camp and Campers' Corner leader. He was what my father would have called an out-and-out soul-winner. He said to me at 11+ time, 'Wouldn't you like to be saved before you start your new school?' This was the Sunday before I started on Monday!

Returning home after the evening gospel meeting, I related to my parents what Howard had said. My father then read to me Isaiah 53:5:

"But He was wounded for our [in effect, my, i.e. David Elson's] *transgressions, He was bruised for our* [my] *iniquities: the chastisement of our peace* [that is, He was punished for my / our sins that we might have them forgiven, and be at peace with God] *was upon him; and with his stripes we are healed."*

Putting my own name into that verse and making it so personal enabled me to repeat the verse in faith, inserting my own name. Later, I was baptised and following that event was received into the church. This all took place in 1943.

GBENGA FAGBENLE (Nigeria)

I am a native of Ibadan, Oyo State, Nigeria. I grew up attending the Church of God in Beyerunka, Ibadan, and later the church moved to Gbelekale, Ibadan. At Sunday School I was taught about Jesus, and memorised many verses of the Bible in order to get a gift of a booklet, although I didn't understand the meaning behind them. Father and mother were members of the church. In June 1994 my father died and went to be with his Saviour and Lord in heaven.

After my primary education, in 1976 I came to Lagos to continue my studies and lived with my uncle and his wife, Mr & Mrs Solomon Ajayi, members of the Church of God in Surulere, Lagos. Here in Lagos I continued to attend church meetings. There was a gospel service every Sunday evening which I went to; by this time I had learned a good bit about Jesus Christ and God's love to mankind, but I never really understood anything about being 'born-again.' One day, Papa Travi, an evangelist in the church, gave an invitation to anyone enquiring about baptism to go and see him. I went with my friend Bernard Obi.

He interviewed Bernard who did well with his answers, but I didn't. I was asked to visit Papa Travi in his home where he gave me a number of scriptural references to help me understand about salvation. I went through them thoroughly. Then one night in 1979 I was at a gospel service when the speaker dealt at length with the subject of 'being born-again'; it was as if he was talking to me personally. When I got home that night, I surrendered to Jesus Christ, accepting Him as my personal Saviour. After a time I was interviewed by 3 elders of the church regarding baptism, and was duly baptised and added to the

Church of God in Surulere in 1980. Glory be to God for His leading and guidance.

FREDA FISHER (Scotland)

I came to the Lord Jesus in January 1934 when I was 13 years of age. That night I was affected by a gospel message given by Dr Mandelson who asked if any in the audience wanted to be saved. After the meeting ended a few of us approached him, and after 'a chat', I accepted the Lord Jesus as my personal Saviour. I was so happy that I ran home and told my family about my decision.

I kept going to Bible Class on Sundays. I was so fond of the cinema yet stopped going for about a year, feeling it was wrong. One day, passing the picture hall I saw the film that was on, 'Rebecca of Sunnybrook Farm', so I went in and returned to my old ways. My mum was upset that I had gone back. I still knew I was saved though.

The night war broke out in 1939 I was out walking with a friend when I met Violet Edgar, who was friendly with my companion, so I invited both of them to accompany me to the Bible Classes I attended. Violet was very interested and that got us to attend other meetings and eventually Violet trusted the Saviour herself. I lost the desire for the cinema and as time went on became very interested in church meetings and asked for baptism in Wyndford Hall, Maryhill, Glasgow. They did not have a baptismal tank, so they said Violet and I could be received into the church and would be baptised later. After about 2 months we went back to the elders of that meeting and told them we should not have been received into the church when we were not baptised! So, shortly after that we were baptised in another hall – Springburn Gospel Hall, as it had a tank.

A few years later I heard about Churches of God, known to some of us by this time as 'Needed Truth.' A man called Mr Beattie, who belonged to the Church of God in Glasgow, Cathcart Road company, gave us a talk on the Scriptures. Violet and I were very interested in what he was saying about church truth. As a result we began attending meetings in another company of the Church of God in Glasgow which was in Partick, and after 3 months or so we were both received into fellowship there, where we were very happy. That was in September 1948. For many years now, after marriage, I have been numbered with the Church of God in Bathgate.

ROGER FISHER (England)

While sitting in a gospel meeting in Halifax, my home town, I had a strong feeling that it was wrong, in a way, that Jesus should be crucified on the cross as He was innocent of any crime and was without any sin. In my mind, I spoke to Him there and then, as if He was hanging there, and said something along the lines of, 'Jesus, it's not right that you should be up there; come down and punish all these people that are treating you so wrongfully.' Later, while in Leeds looking for a new suit for a wedding at which I was to be best man for a footballing friend, I came across two people distributing leaflets in a shopping precinct. Feeling uncomfortable, I tried to avoid them, but I felt like being reeled in like a fish on a hook and drawn towards them.

Taking a leaflet, I had a talk with them. They explained the message of the leaflet more fully. I knew I needed to speak with God about my sin and ask for forgiveness, realising that Jesus had died on the cross for me. They suggested I should say a prayer as I was leaving them. I asked them to write me one as we were out on the street and I couldn't get down on my knees there! I knew the 'Lord's Prayer' and 'churchy' formal prayers, but I wanted to speak personally to God, but did not have the words. I promised them that if they wrote one I would say that prayer when I got home. I meant that statement seriously, more than I had ever said anything in my life; I needed to do it.

When I got home I said the prayer, thanking Jesus for dying for me and asking forgiveness for all my sins. Nothing happened for a time until next evening, while watching television, the words of a hymn suddenly became real to me and I knew God had forgiven me, and I cried with joy. I was so overwhelmed with a deep sense of God's love for me.

The most marvellous thing is I got 2 new suits! The one for the wedding has long worn away, but the one Jesus gave me when I accepted Him as my Saviour will never wear away! It fits me for ever. I am clothed in the righteousness of Christ, free from the guilt of my sin, and made right before God, because of Christ's sacrifice for me. A verse which sums it all up for me is, *"For He* [God] *made Him who knew no sin* [Christ] *to be sin for us, that we might become the righteousness of God in Him"* (2 Corinthians 5:21).

JACKY FORBES (Scotland)

The first words of the Bible to take root in my heart are found in Revelation 20:1-2: *"And I saw an angel coming down out of heaven, having the key of the abyss and a great chain in his hand. And he laid hold on the dragon, the old serpent, which is the Devil and Satan, and bound him for a thousand years."*

You might think these words are not ones in which a person could see the great love which God has for everyone. You see, I always believed Satan was a very real being and was man's deadliest enemy. The reasons for my conviction will become obvious as my story unfolds.

I was the second eldest of a family of 4: 3 boys and 1 girl. The girl was the youngest. My father was in the theatrical business and though his main occupation was as a booking agent, he was no mean performer on the stage and topped the bill in virtually all the bigger halls in the country and also Canada. Our family situation was not a happy one. Dad made a great deal of money but none of it found its way into the home. He needed every penny he could earn, beg, borrow or steal; he was an alcoholic. At times he even seemed to be demon-possessed. I could never tell all the misery and unhappiness that was caused by the power of the bottle of whisky, which was his only master. Thankfully, because of the nature of his work, he was away from the family for long periods. We often went hungry. Likewise, the clothes we wore were those provided by the authorities for families like ours - with no money around. I have never forgotten how my poor mother managed to keep her sanity as I reflect on some of the dreadful things that took place in our home. The laws of decency prevent me from detailing disgusting scenes as men and women of the theatre spent whole nights at our place in drunken debauchery.

Father was also violent. Beatings took place all the time he was at home. He was able to instil fear into every fibre of our bodies. We had no toys. Our prized possession was a cat we all loved dearly. However, my father hated anything that was the object of love, and one night, in spite of all our protests and tears, he took the cat and put it in the oven, closing the door and turning on the gas. After the noise inside the oven subsided he pulled the cat out and left it for dead, laughing hilariously at his devilish joke. As a very young lad I was often roughly shaken in the middle of the night while in bed. Many times I have wondered what thoughts troubled him as he kept repeating 'There is no God! There is no God! It was me that gave you life.' When left alone at last, I wondered if there was a God in heaven. I had no doubts there was a Devil! I knew he was real for sure.

One day my older brother, at the age of 14, dared to stand against my father. He was taken through to the bedroom, stripped, and savagely beaten. As I looked on his face there wasn't a tear in his eye, only a look of bewilderment. If I had been able that day, as a boy of 12, I would have killed my father where he stood. Instead of the fear it should have instilled within me, the seeds of murder were sown in my heart. I only lived for the day when I would be old and strong enough to wreak my vengeance upon this man who was my father.

At 14 I was in work and returned home one Friday with the few shillings in my wage packet. He confronted me for the money to be handed over to him. I refused. Well, he got my wages alright and it was 2 weeks before I was able to return to work. At the age of 20, I came home one night to find my sister and mother crying their eyes out. They told me what happened. The years of hatred and resentment welled up in me and I look back on that day, seeing my father in a welter of his own blood, after I went for him. It was one of the blackest days of my life, for as I stood there looking at his helplessness, I saw myself as a potential murderer if ever there was one. Only by God's grace that murder was not committed that day.

The home broke up as a result. My mother disappeared and, unknown to me, obtained a divorce and remarried. I wasn't to see her for another 10 years and, even when I did see her, she had a new husband and family and did not want to have anything to do with her old life or anything that reminded her of it. I told her that in the intervening years I had received Christ as my own and personal Saviour. I thanked God for the semblance of happiness she now possessed and hoped and prayed that she too would find salvation.

My father also remarried and his second wife could stick it out for only a few months when she ended it all by suicide. He went down south and wherever he is, I pray that the Lord will cast the demon out of him and save his soul. Shortly after the home broke up I changed my job to employment with Butters Brothers in Govan, Glasgow. There I worked beside a man called Bob Jarvie, who was a Christian. For the first time in my life I came under the sound of the gospel. I heard the wonderful story of redemption; how God sent his Son into the world to die for sinners like me. Sad to say, initially, the words of eternal life had no effect on me. From that job I was called up to the forces and spent time in Germany. While in the army I married a girl whom I had known in my early teens. For the first time in my life I was shown what a real home could be like: no hate or violence. Nothing would now deprive me of this precious thing which I now possessed. I would fight for it with all the resources I could muster.

I was then 'demobbed' from the army and found my way back to Butters Brothers. There Bob Jarvie was still testifying to God's grace. I listened to all his stories from the Bible. One day he spoke of how Satan the Devil would be chained for a thousand years and of how Christ would reign over the whole world. No longer would the drunkard or sadist be free to wreak havoc. No more wars. Harmony even in the animal realm where the wolf would lie down with the lamb. My heart leaped when hearing there was One who was mightier than Satan. From that moment, I determined I would become part of this soon-coming kingdom. I returned home that night, read the book of Revelation and started on the gospels. The more I read the deeper I came under conviction. Even returning from work, I would reach for the Bible before eating my meal. Then one night my wife, Cathy, burst out 'I can't stand this any longer! You will have to choose between the Bible and me.'

Oh, how I recognised the Evil One. He was attacking me in my only vulnerable spot: the sanctity of my own home. I was sorely tempted to close the book I was coming to love, never to open it again. But I decided to trust God. I told my darling wife I would have to keep searching until I discovered this well of life. And God upheld me. From that moment my wife came under deep conviction and together we tried to work out our own salvation with fear and trembling. For weeks on end we went to gospel meetings and at the end the preacher would try to lead us to the Saviour. Then, one morning at work I came to the glorious realisation that Jesus had died for me, came into my life and entered my heart. I knew I was well and truly saved. It was with some misgivings I knocked on my home door that night, not knowing how to break the news to my unsaved wife. Imagine my great surprise when she told me that she too had been saved that very day: her in the home and me at work. What a wonderful Saviour is Jesus my Lord.

Just 18 months ago we were preparing to go on holiday with our 5-year-old son. He took ill from an unknown malady. Within a week, instead of holidaying with him we were burying him. Our world crumbled. I tell you, friend, if we had not the Lord Jesus to comfort us in all our sorrow we would both have finished our journey in life there and then. The promise of the Lord is not that trouble and affliction will disappear entirely from our lives, but He will comfort and sustain us to carry on, no matter what lies before.

Why don't you take Him now? You will have a friend like no other who will never leave or forsake you. May the Lord bless you and give you deciding grace today, to accept Him before it's too late to do so.

PETER FORSYTH (Scotland)

On reflection, the day of my birth was not one of rejoicing, rather one of anxiety. In her pregnancy my mother was very ill with pre-eclampsia, and both she and father were told not to expect me to survive. My birth was premature and I was placed on a cold slab, which was indicative that there was no life in me. This was 79 years ago when the expertise and technology that is around today was not available. Fortunately, a passing doctor heard a whimper from me and, realising there was life in the little frame, made a positive attempt to resuscitate me. I was then put in an incubator. I weighed 2lbs 10 oz. and was 14 inches long. Normal baby weights in those days, I am told, was 7–8 lbs and length 19–20 inches. It was said to me many times later that my face at birth was no larger than a gentleman's pocket watch! In those times, it was considered a miracle if such a tiny baby survived at all. As a testimony to that, a picture of me at that stage was hung in the corridor of the Simpson Memorial Hospital in Edinburgh.

As time went by, it was noted I was making no attempt to walk and was eventually diagnosed with cerebral palsy. I needed a lot of tender loving care. Mother was advised if she had any more children she would be unable to provide the care and attention I required daily. I am grateful to this day for all the love and devotion she selflessly lavished on me. *"From a babe you have known the sacred writings which are able to make you wise unto salvation through faith in Christ Jesus"* (2 Timothy 3:15). I was very fortunate to have Christian parents who loved God's word, the sacred scriptures. Regularly on Sunday evenings, following the gospel service, church friends of my parents would meet in one of their homes for a time of singing around the piano or organ. There was no television in those times and folks were just glad to sit around and talk over the Scriptures. A favourite topic was 'The Coming of the Lord.'

While I would mostly be playing on the carpet with my dinky cars, little by little I began to understand what was being said. This would conjure up in my mind pictures of cars crashing and planes falling out of the skies when Jesus came back to the air for all who had believed on Him as their Saviour. I also thought of the pilot who was a Christian being taken to heaven at the Lord's return, and passengers who were not Christians having their lives come to a swift end and no longer having the possibility of obtaining eternal life by trusting Christ as their Saviour.

Around the age of 9 I was very conscious that I was not saved, and the thought of the Lord returning and me being left behind was a terrifying one. This fear was compounded by the thought of my parents being taken away and my dependency on them being removed. Such thoughts greatly troubled me until one Sunday evening, lying in bed, I got up and fetched my Bible, opening it at John 3:16, a verse I knew by heart at this time. I read the verse over and over, then the whole chapter. The last verse stood out: *"He/she that believes on the Son has eternal life; but he/she that obeys not the Son shall not see life, but the wrath of God abides on them."* I didn't like these words at all, and hastily turned the pages. My eye caught John 5:24: *"Verily, verily, the person that hears my word, and believes Him that sent me, has eternal life, and comes not into judgement, but has passed out of death into life."* These words were similar to John 3:16, I thought. Suddenly, the realisation flooded into my mind and I knew that if I simply took God at His word I would be saved eternally.

Nobody was with me, but I knew with absolute certainty that God had now saved me. I didn't tell anyone for a while. However, a few months later on a Sunday evening after supper, my mother said, 'Would you like to be saved, son?', to which I replied, 'But, I am saved, mother.'

'Why did you not tell us?' she asked. 'I didn't like to,' I replied. Tears of joy were visible in Mum and Dad's eyes. Interestingly, I came to appreciate the words of Romans 10:9 and the need to openly confess the Lord Jesus to others, telling them of salvation and faith. That strengthens one's own faith and gives an impetus to go forward in Christian life.

At the age of 12 the Lord put into my heart the desire to be baptised and follow Him in my life. I asked about this to mother and father, and also to my grandfather, Mr David Richardson. I was interviewed by two of the elders in the Church of God in Broxburn, one being my Uncle George Richardson, the other the husband of my mother's cousin, Mr Harry Dyer. There was concern over my fragile health in being submerged in water, though only for a couple of seconds. My mother had the answer when the matter was discussed with my parents: 'The God who can save my bairn, can bring him through the waters of baptism.' I was baptised the following Sunday by my father, not because I was his son, but because he had that duty in the assembly. It was an unforgettable experience. As I came up out of the water, my face was beaming. I sang myself to sleep that night with the words of the hymn, "Oh happy day, that fixed my choice, on Thee my Saviour and my God!" I was then added to the Church of God in Broxburn, part of 'The Fellowship of the Son of God,' and have sought ever since to be faithful to the Lord.

I would particularly like to mention the name of Mr Douglas Mair, who for many years was my 'spiritual father' and helped greatly in my coming to understand the Lord's teaching.

BERNARD FRENCH (England)

From the age of 4, I attended the Sunday School at the Church of God in Crowborough, East Sussex. Later I was in the Bible Class, which was run by Mr Jesse Taylor. Although my parents were not believers at that time, they encouraged my brothers and me to be regular at these classes. I learnt a lot and enjoyed stories from the Bible, but had no thought of salvation.

For years the Churches of God have organised Bible Camps and in August 1945 I went to my first one at Shoreham in Sussex. I had a head knowledge of the way of salvation, but with many friends and interests, I had no wish to change anything. August 15th that year was a celebration of America's victory over Japan and there was tremendous excitement everywhere. Rather than go to the evening talk in the camp I pleaded a headache and went to my tent. Geoff Mutimer, a worker there, followed me and quietly read some scriptures. I particularly remember John 3:16 and Romans 10:9. He asked if I would like to be saved. I knew that expression and its meaning, and said I would. 'I'll leave you now', he said, and walked out of the tent. I knelt on the mattress and began to recite the Lord's Prayer, but after a couple of sentences I said, 'God, that's not what I want to say'. I broke down and there and then received the Lord Jesus Christ as my personal Saviour. A great feeling of joy and peace came over me. Even then I felt everything had been leading up to this moment. I ran out of the tent and shouted, 'I've done it!' Geoff heard me and said, 'Now go and tell someone'. In the darkness I saw Mr Fred Evans coming up the field, and running towards him, I said, 'Mr Evans, I've just got saved.'

In the morning I sent a card to Mr & Mrs Jesse Taylor telling them about my salvation. Now, all things I had learned previously seemed to fall into place. Three months afterwards I was baptised and added to the Church of God in Crowborough. For me, there has never been a day to equal the day I accepted the Lord Jesus into my life. In spite of much failure on my part, He has remained faithful. He is a friend more dear than a brother and He is my Lord, "whose I am and whom I serve." As the years have passed, I thank God for the many who, with faithful testimony and prayers, have been the instruments under God to lead me to everlasting life through faith and show me the true way of discipleship from His word.

BRIAN FULLARTON (Scotland)

'He turned to me'; 'He lifted me'; 'He gave me'; 'as a result many will see and fear and put their trust in the Lord' (Psalm 40:1-3 New International Version of the Bible).

These words above, I feel, are what the Lord has done in my life. My mother and father, and both sets of grandparents, were all believers in the Lord Jesus as their personal Saviour. Both my grandfathers had remarkable 'conversions', one on the football field, the other on the battlefield. They also sought in their lives to bear testimony of what Jesus had done for them, and meant to them. I was very close to my maternal grandparents who were overjoyed to have a grandson after having three daughters! From them I learned the stories of the Bible. My grandfather was Sunday School Superintendent (a big title in those days) at the Open Brethren meeting called 'Chapel Street Hall,' in Barrhead, Renfrewshire, Scotland, where I lived.

I attended Sunday School every week and God used a man called Ivy Speirs to bring conviction of my sin at an early age. He often read Ecclesiastes 3:11 – *"He has set eternity in their heart"* (Revised Version) and spoke of the dreadful possibility of spending eternity without those who loved us if we did not do something about the sin in our hearts that God detested, although loving us so much. This repeatedly gave me great concern even as a youngster.

Then a year or two later, one Saturday morning, being sent to my maternal grandmother to run an errand for her, I opened the door of her house and I could hear her praying - for me! I can't remember what she said, but the fact that she was praying so earnestly on my behalf made a deep impression on my young heart. In this respect I often think of the words of Ecclesiastes 9:17: *"The quiet words of the wise are more to be heeded than the shouts of a ruler."*

The final step that led to my trusting the Saviour completely and having the assurance of my sins being forgiven was at the Billy Graham 'Tell Scotland Campaign' in 1955, held in the Kelvin Hall arena in Glasgow. The famous words of John 3:16 rang out loudly in my heart one particular night. I knew beyond doubt that Jesus loved me, died for me, and only He could save me for ever.

When I was sixteen years of age I was very reluctant, but gently persuaded, to go to a Bible Class that was held in the house of a man called Mr Ferguson at his home that went by the name of 'Ferndean.' Since my conversion I had not been interested in making anything of my life in terms of Christian service or commitment. Going to 'Uncle Jack' & 'Aunt Olga's' residence on Sunday afternoons changed all that. At 17 I went for a week to the Churches of God Camp at Auchenfoyle camp site near Kilmacolm. Harry King, giving lessons from Guy Jarvie's book 'The Life Indeed,' greatly influenced me and I decided to follow the Lord Jesus as best as I could with the help of God and was soon baptised and added to the Church of God in Barrhead.

I soon came to realise in my early twenties that the Churches of God in the Fellowship of the Son of God, a worldwide movement, was not just another church in which God could be served, but a very special testimony to Him where His name could be honoured by disciples serving together according to the pattern of His word. This was the place where He wanted me to be for the rest of the days of my life (Psalm 23:6b).

JOAN FULLARTON (Scotland)

I was born 24th May, 1945, in a nursing home called 'Kingsmeadows' in Peebles, in the Borders area of Scotland. I was the eldest of 6 children born to Frank and Dolly Smith. One of the family, Pamela, died at the age of 3 months. Dad and Mum were both from Lancashire, England and when Dad took his stance as a 'conscientious objector' in the early 1940s, he was sent into forestry work, which brought him up to the Borders. When this work finished he then became a chauffeur for a time, before finding a job in the Textile industry as a 'carder.' For a few years he attended night school classes and eventually became a Lecturer at Galashiels College of Textiles, which later became part of Heriot-Watt University in Edinburgh.

Mum and Dad were Christians and, with a few other folk in the area, were members of the Church of God in Innerleithen, which was a small town of under 2,000 people. Here they resided and brought up the family. I came to know the Lord Jesus as my personal Saviour at the age of 10, having listened to many Bible stories, especially about the Lord Jesus and His love. John chapter 3, verse 16, was the verse that gave me assurance of salvation. Dad was responsible for the Sunday School, and all the boys and girls knew our family well, as did other townsfolk. At the age of 11, I understood that the Lord Jesus was baptised and it was His will and desire that those who believed on Him should do the same, as a witness to having taken Him into our lives. That took place in a Mill dam that flowed just behind the main street in the town. I remember it was raining and cold. I then became part of the congregation of the church, as I saw this was the next step I should take as a disciple of

Jesus Christ. One by one my brothers, and sister, took the same steps as followers of Jesus.

What was difficult for me was going out every Sunday evening before the 'inside' gospel meeting held in the hall, and standing in the streets of the town with those in the church, holding what we called 'open-air meetings.' Dad and a friend in the church called Jock Bell, a foreman in one of the textile factories nearby, preached the gospel at every street corner in the town over the years. Everybody knew who we were, so it wasn't easy to do. Some people laughed, others shook their heads at us doing this, because we also sang hymns – without musical accompaniment and only the voices of a few folk of the church. That went on for many years.

At High School in Peebles, I enjoyed hockey, eventually captaining the team. On leaving school, my burning desire was to go into the nursing profession, but my parents felt this was not the right choice of career for me. It would mean I would not be able to be at the 'Breaking of Bread' in church every Sunday, keeping the 'Remembrance' of the Lord Jesus, acknowledging the great sacrifice He made for all of us in laying down His life for our sins so that we might be forgiven, and receive the gift of everlasting life. That was a disappointment to me, but later I secured a post at Peel Hospital near Clovenfords as a Medical Secretary, doing secretarial and administrative work for two physicians: Drs. Borthwick and Clark. I thoroughly enjoyed working in the hospital environment, and this was the first of a variety of secretarial roles during my working life.

After meeting Brian and starting our courtship in Bangor, Northern Ireland, and eventually marrying, we moved to Ayrshire. Our daughter Claire was born there before we moved back to 'my home territory' in the Borders; later our son Maurice was born. As the children reached their teens they too followed the same pattern as Brian and myself, which gave us great joy. Many years later we set up home in East Lothian for a short time, before 'landing' in West Lothian, where we have been for 22 years. We are still associated with Churches of God, where we believe the Lord would have us serve Him. Now with 5 grandchildren ranging in age from 5-16, we can look back in thankfulness for God's grace to us and love for us, and joyfully sing:

"All the way my Saviour leads me; what have I to ask beside?
Can I doubt His tender mercy, who through life has been my Guide?
Heavenly peace, divinest comfort, here by faith in Him to dwell;
For I know, whate'er befall me, Jesus doeth all things well."
(Fanny Crosby)

LANG ZA GIN (Myanmar)

I was born on 30th December, 1945, in Suangphei Village. My parents were Christians. From early childhood I was aware of the grievance of my mother because of my defective legs. One day she said to me, 'My son, if you die in unbelief you must go to hell. But Jesus died to save you to bring you to God, that you might not go there.' That very day I received the Lord Jesus as my personal Saviour. How happy I was. I was baptised in the Baptist church in 1963, but later joined the Church of God in Suangphei in 1968. Then I moved to Munlai where a church of God was planted in 1977. By God's grace I have served God as an elder in both churches.

DAVID GRAY (Scotland)

I was one of three boys born to Isaac and Mary Gray. We lived on a small holding well off the main bus route. We had some livestock, but growing fresh fruit was the main income of the family. Our home was a place where God's word was read and taught. As young lads we were familiar with the stories of the Bible from an early age. Each Sunday we were taken to the services of the Church of God in Crossford. There we learned of sin and man's disobedience, and also of God's great love in giving His Son, the Lord Jesus, to die on the cross to take away our sin.

It was at one of the gospel meetings there in October 1947 that something very special happened. The preacher, Mr Harry Brindle, read John 3:16 and invited us to make it very personal by putting our own name into the verse, so that it read as follows: "For God so loved [David Gray], that He have His only begotten Son, that if [David Gray] believes on Him, [David Gray] would not perish, but have eternal life." Unknown to me, or anyone else in the hall, my elder brother Tom, who was sitting beside me, was convicted of his sin, did what the preacher asked, and was saved during the meeting. After the service, my father and Tom hurried on to visit my grandparents who lived nearby, while mother, younger brother, Isaac, and I walked the mile home at a leisurely pace. It was now 8:00 p.m. and being winter, it was dark. I changed out of my 'Sunday best' to go and bring in my pet goat.

Usually I would just call for her and she would come, but not that night. Eventually, I realised something was wrong and after searching discovered she had strangled herself with her chain. As a distraught

11-year-old I ran to mother, breaking my heart at the loss of my dear pet. Having consoled me, she reminded me of Mr Brindle's message about God's love, the possibility of perishing and the invitation to put my name into the verse and accepting the Lord Jesus as my personal Saviour. Sitting on her knee, she asked me the question, 'If it had been you who died tonight, where would you have gone?' I knew the answer full well, having heard the gospel story many times. There in that room, I thanked God for loving me, confessed my sin, and believed that Jesus died for David Gray. I was saved.

Shortly afterwards, the door opened and in came father and Tom. 'Mary, I've got great news for you', Father said, his face beaming, 'Tom got saved during the service tonight'. Mother then said to him, 'Isaac, I've got great news for you; David has just got saved sitting on my knee." Luke 15:10 says, *"Even so, I say unto you, there is joy in the presence of the angels of God over one sinner that repents."*

GILBERT GRIERSON (England)

I'd like to give a heading to my story. It is 'From Pots to Peace.' It begins at Wetheriggs Pottery, Cumbria in 1972 where I was an apprentice training in the skills of craft pottery-making, with the hope of taking over the business from the retiring owner. However, I have a terrible dilemma. I have just come to realise that this world will not go on for ever; that terrible times lie ahead that affect everybody. I understand where humankind is heading and what will be the ultimate effect of globalisation. I am convinced there will be an economic and social breakdown within my lifetime. It makes me very pessimistic, and although it is a tough decision, I decide to ditch my pottery plans and dreams.

Now back in Yorkshire, where I was born, I find work on a farm. I share my views about where the world is going with a fellow-worker. He tells me the Bible speaks of terrible times ahead. This is news to me. He also says that Jesus Christ is coming back again and we have to keep God's commandments to be saved from perishing. He further states the 4th commandment is that we should keep the Sabbath Day, and do no work on it. He shows me that the 7th day, the biblical sabbath , runs from Friday evening until Saturday evening, as observed by the Jewish people. I am not sure what to believe. One thing I do know is that I have broken God's commandments and am a sinner. As a boy I stole fruit and told lies, and much more besides as I grew older. I try to clean up my life and start to read the Bible.

After 3 years I decide to go Israel for a year and work on a collective farm (or 'kibbutz'). My reasoning is, 'If Jesus is really coming back for those who obey Him, then the best place to be is Israel, and try to keep God's commandments there.' I arrive in the Valley of Jezreel, which runs down to the Jordan Valley, in January 1975. I carry a little red Gideon's Bible, given me when I left school aged 16 in Yorkshire. When I was young I never used to think about God despite going to Sunday School and church. Now I am looking for answers and for peace. My jobs that year include picking grapefruit, irrigating cotton, working in a plastics factory, and later on in Jerusalem, working in a small tile-making workshop in the old city, and also in a salami sausage-making shop.

On the kibbutz I often pray and read the Bible. I learn Hebrew and go on trips to the Golan Heights, the Dead Sea, and to Eilat on the Red Sea. Most of my friends are Jewish. They don't talk about Jesus. Inside I want to believe in God and Jesus, because I see this as the only hope for the world. I don't understand the gospel or how to be 'saved' and cannot find anyone to explain it to me. I think you have to do certain things and live in a certain way, and this will make a person acceptable to God when Jesus returns. I fast and pray a lot that year; once all night on the Jewish Day of Atonement ('Yom Kippur') up Mount Gilboa just behind the kibbutz.

I make one special friend in 1975; a Jewish girl from Russia called Tamara. We learn Hebrew together in a class for new immigrants and volunteers. I am a volunteer, but she had come from Russia and settled in Israel with her sister. We converse in simple Hebrew. We spend a lot of time together, but Tamara does not know the battle going on inside me. It is too difficult to explain. If there is no God, there is no hope! One day I make up my mind to trust in God and also trust that if Tamara comes back to England with me, things will work out. We make our plans, but she is Jewish, with no belief in Jesus whom Jews do not accept as their Messiah. Many are taught to hate His name. But I am secretly trying to follow Jesus' example, hoping this will save me.

One day in November I head off to Jerusalem alone. A crisis has occurred in my friendship with Tamara. I have hit rock bottom! My life is a complete failure. I can't go on any longer. I am physically weak and mentally exhausted; at the end of my tether. In desperation I walk through the streets of the city, thinking all the time. I had tried to do all the right things. I had carried a heavy burden on my own. There was no one to help. Suddenly a thought hits me. Why am I trying to be good enough for God and keep all His commandments? Jesus had come and had done it for me. He had lived a perfect life and fulfilled the law perfectly. He had also given Himself up as a sacrifice. None other was needed. I had shut out His help. What God has to give – salvation – is free; a gift. It only has to be received! That day in Jerusalem I find what I am looking for. I am set free. A great weight lifts from my life. There is nothing to do: only believe and receive, and go on to live a new life to the full. God will take care of the future. Everything is in His hands. I experience the 'new birth.'

I leave Israel in 1976. I never see Tamara again (later she marries a Jewish man from Russia). Back in England I discover a new life as a Christian. I meet and have fellowship with others who believe the same things. I come into contact with disciples of the Lord Jesus in the Church of God in Leeds, Yorkshire. I get baptised as a disciple by immersion and added to the local church of God in June 1977. The Lord has given me a new life. Five years later he gives me Sue, my lovely wife. He gives us a son, Danny, now also a disciple. He gives us purpose in life. He is patient and true. And this is my story which He gives to you. 'What will you do with Jesus?' 3 lessons:

1. Sin is sin. It doesn't change. It is serious.
2. God is God. He doesn't change. He is holy. He must punish sin. He is also Love. He has a plan to save sinners.
3. Jesus is Jesus. He is the same in 1975 and today. His salvation is the same. He took the sinner's place. He is ready to save.

P.S. I still carry in my pocket the same little red Gideon's Bible: getting quite battered now!

SUE GRIERSON (England)

As far as I can remember, there was never a time when I didn't believe in the God of all creation. At a very early age I had a great desire to be a nun! I used to admire their gracefulness and quietness and what they did for others. I also loved stories and films about missionaries. Anything to do with God held great appeal for me. I was taken to Sunday School along with my brothers and at the age of 12 I learned a verse that I believe was my 'salvation text' – John 3:16. During the next 2 years my parents' marriage broke down and they left the church they had been attending. However, at 14 years of age I knew that I wanted to obey the Lord Jesus, and having believed on Him as my Saviour, to be baptised, which I did. This took place at Alleyne Road Hall, which was the meeting place of the Church of God in Birmingham. After that, because of what happened with my parents, I drifted away from church. One thing I do recall though is praying to God every night. For the next 10 years I never went near a church and at 23 got a job in London as a nanny, and so left home.

It was during my year in London that the Lord began to work in my life again. I bought a Bible and for some reason I was directed to Jeremiah 31:3 - a wonderful verse God has often used in other lives too, *"I have loved you with an everlasting love; I have drawn you with lovingkindness."* Yes, He was bringing me back to Himself. I had gone away from Him. So I began my service for Him in His dwelling-place on earth – the House of God.

In 1977 I met a young man at work who belonged to the 'Open Brethren' movement. I prayed so hard for him to come into the Church of God in Birmingham, but it didn't seem to be happening and this caused me great sadness, even to the extent I was ready to leave my church and go along to his. Because I wanted to be absolutely certain that I was serving God in the right place, I set myself to search the Scriptures about the truth of God's house and that truth became very precious to me. At the end of that year the Lord brought our relationship to an end. This broke my heart and for the next 2 years my faithful God poured in the healing oil.

Then in 1979 I met my husband Gilbert at a Tent Gospel Campaign in Birmingham. By this time the Lord had healed and blessed me so much. We lived in Leeds for 9 years and our son Dan was born. Then we moved to Barrow-in-Furness where the Lord gave us the privilege and responsibility of looking after a small assembly with a big youth work. Sadly, after 10 years the assembly had to close with only 3 of us left there, and the youth work had to stop: though we haven't stopped praying for them! Some years later we moved over to Northern Ireland and have been involved in helping a small assembly - the Church of God in Knocknacloy. God is the great Healer of our lives. While we have been here the Lord has been working with me, clearing out of my life things that are of no use to Him. My everyday desire is to be well-pleasing to Him in every area of my life. Times alone with Him are precious. I know that my day depends on my God. Two verses of a poem by Mrs E. Cowman are very special to me:

"Still, still with You, when the purple morning breaks,
When the birds awake, and the shadows flee;
Fairer than morning, lovelier than daylight,
Dawns the sweet consciousness, I am with Thee."
"Alone with You, amid the misty shadows,
The solemn hush of nature newly born;
Alone with You in breathless adoration,
In the calm dew and freshness of the morn."

My mother came back into the assembly. My brothers trusted in the Lord Jesus and also became part of the Church of God in Birmingham.

PETER HAGENBUCH (England)

I was born in 1954. My parents brought me up in the church; my dad was a lay preacher. However, I did not have a strong faith and when I left home in 1972 I stopped going to church and did not go back for nearly 20 years. I got married (in church!) in 1983 and my wife and I moved to Scotland in 1986. Our second child was very ill as a baby and we nearly lost her at 6 weeks; following surgery she stopped breathing for 20 minutes. I was told the medics had 'given up' on her - then she started breathing again. We decided we would like her baptised as we thought she might not live for long. The hospital chaplain baptised her then turned to us with a smile and said 'you might be surprised how babies sometimes pick up after being baptized!' Thirty-two years later she is still with us, with multiple health issues but a blessing and inspiration to many.

We decided to put our daughters into Sunday School; we were not churchgoers, but it seemed like the right thing to do. The church encouraged the parents to go to a 'Family Service' once a month and my wife and I went along without any great enthusiasm. However, I found to my surprise that I enjoyed the services and the preaching. I started going to church every week and I could see that some people in the church 'had something' which I did not have. I reached a stage where I wanted to believe. On Easter Day, 1992 the service seemed to be just for me: the hymns, one of which was, "I serve a risen Saviour," and the preaching – from John's gospel chapter 20:24-29 – *"stop doubting and believe,"* left me in tears for most of the service and I came to a strong faith which has never left me.

I became an enthusiastic Christian, which did not go down well at home. My wife accused me of caring more about the church than about my own family. As the years went by my wife had an increasing amount of anger in her and I was the main target. Social Work got involved and decided that my wife and I should separate for the sake of our younger daughter. I agreed to move out although I did not feel I was at fault. I did not have any savings and I contemplated sleeping rough; then I thought 'I'm a Christian now, I should pray about this.' I woke up remembering a charity I had helped 15 years before; I knew they had an empty building and I asked if I could stay there. They agreed and let me stay there for free.

Separation seemed like a disaster at first, but I found I had some freedom to make decisions which I did not have before. I applied to go to Honduras with the Tearfund 'Transform' programme – the idea is that you are transformed by the experience of living and working alongside some very poor people. I needed £1,350 to go and I had no savings but I felt that the money would come from somewhere, which it did - the exact amount!

This led to me learning Spanish and sponsoring my first child with 'Compassion.' As the years went by I got involved with projects for children in Uruguay and Brazil. In 2014, 11 years after my separation, I was in a big church in Brazil with a Brazilian friend. There were about 2000 people in the church and I was about 10 rows from the front. The pastor pointed to me amongst these 2000 people and asked me (in Portuguese, which I had learned) to see him after the service. He told me that something amazing was going to happen in my family and he asked if he could pray for me.

When I got back to Scotland, my wife, who had been angry with me throughout 11 years of separation, started to soften. She was diagnosed with Alzheimer's and we noticed she was getting very thin; by then she was living on her own. She agreed to let me into the house to cook for her and give her medication. She trusted me with keys for the house, front and back. We renewed our marriage vows in June 2014 and went on a short family holiday with our daughters. Two weeks later my wife had the central heating serviced. The engineer needed a part and agreed to come back Thursday morning. I went along to make sure he got access; I was still living at a separate address. We rang the doorbell, no answer. The front door was bolted so I let myself in at the back. I found my wife lying on her bed; I thought she was dead but she was just alive so I called an ambulance. She had had a stroke; lying there helpless with her life ebbing away, perhaps praying for someone to come.

My wife survived and five years later she is still with us, in a Care Home, disabled by the stroke. Her anger has diminished and a process of reconciliation has taken place in my family, for which I thank God. My wife used to hate me, hate God, hate the church. Now she loves me and loves God and comes happily to church with me. She has accepted Jesus as her Lord and Saviour. She prays for the other residents in the Care Home. God is amazing and I live to serve Him, in Jesus' name!

MARGARET HALPIN (England)

I treasure a small hymnbook, at the front of which is written, 'To Margaret, age 7 years, June 1951, from Daddy and Mummy with love.' Strangely, I was delighted to be given this. Although my brother and I were brought up in a Christian home, I understood, even then, that I personally needed to be saved. One day the following year I was singing by myself from that hymnbook:

"Down from the glory the Saviour came,
Down to the Cross and the death of shame;
Gazing in wonder I there exclaim –
Jesus died for me."
(Anon.)

Suddenly I believed this meant 'me', and I knew then I was saved eternally. Four years later I was baptised and then added to the Churches of God. Knowing I have a God and Saviour, whom I can approach in any circumstances, has been invaluable.

DAVID HANSEN (England)

My brother Robert, aka 'Bob', and I were active members of the Church of England since becoming teenagers. In the early 1950s Bob was transferred, in the course of his employment with Customs & Excise, to the Greenock area of Scotland. There he met a young lady office clerk, and after a while he accompanied her, along with her parents, to a Bible Conference in Edinburgh. One of the speakers was Mr Arthur Jones, an evangelist in the Churches of God. Bob later told me he had 'got saved' and was leaving the Church of England to join what I considered to be no more than a little sect; it was called 'The Churches of God.' He would send me magazines produced by this church, with names like 'Intelligence', 'Bible Studies', and 'Needed Truth.' I read these avidly, with my Bible alongside me, to find the errors of this teaching as I wanted him out of this 'sect.' However, after spending 18 months or so not finding any, I started attending their communion service, which they called 'The Remembrance' or 'The Breaking of Bread.' Their nearest church to me was in Kingston, Surrey. I sat at the back and listened intently to all that was being said. Then, after reading an article by Mr G. Prasher Snr. entitled "The One Place for God", I began to realise these people were right. They were the New Testament equivalent of the early churches of God as recorded in the New Testament of the Bible. In April 1956 I faced the big choice. I became convinced of the truth of the "The Place of God's Name" (Deuteronomy 12:11). I accepted Jesus as my personal Saviour, and soon after that, I was baptised by immersion in water and then added to the believers who were in the Church of God in Kingston.

GO KHUA HAU (Myanmar)

I was born of Christian parents in Suangphei Village, Chin State, Myanmar. I grew up miserably as the Second World War was being fought. One Sunday morning our church pastor spoke of the death of the Lord Jesus for sinners like me. The message so touched my heart that I repented of my sins with tears, and also feeling so upset that my sins had caused Him to go through so much. I was 10 years old and began to love the Saviour and resolved to do my very best for Him in my life. I loved to sing gospel hymns like, "When I survey the wondrous cross"; "Alas! And did my Saviour bleed"; and "I gave my life for thee." Something was still missing though. I did not learn the Bible texts assuring me that I possessed completely eternal life.

At 17 I joined the S.D.A. movement and was baptised on the 17th September, 1957. I thought I'd found the truth. However, I was not satisfied. With the help of a Christian friend, and looking at scriptures like John 5:24; 10:28; Ephesians 2:8-9 and 1 John 5:13, it dawned on me that I was saved eternally the first time I received the Lord Jesus into my life. Now I wanted to proclaim free salvation, but that could not be done within the legalistic Adventist Church. I had to leave it.

I returned to the Baptist Church. They were not satisfied with my baptism in the S.D.A. church, so I was baptised again on the last Sunday of January 1963. It was during those days my uncle, Tual Khaw Zam, showed me booklets written by Mr Guy Jarvie, who was an evangelist belonging to the Churches of God. I wrote a letter to Mr Jarvie. He replied at once. There were many discussions about his booklets and one day I read U Thein Maung's "Why I worship in a church of God" to our old pastor. He was not slow to believe the teaching and said, 'I will join the church of God even if I am alone'; which he did (in Suangphei) and was known as Brother Kim Za Kap.

In 1966 my Baptist friends sent me to meet Mr Jarvie in Insein. I invited 2 other friends from Tedim town. We spent a week with him in early February. My 2 friends did not grasp the truth we were being taught, so we parted company in Rangoon. I returned home to Suangphei. On arriving I was greatly surprised to find that several friends had withdrawn from the Baptist church, for the sake of being obedient to the truth of God as the Churches of God taught. These men were the nucleus of the church of God that was planted in Suangphei on 15th May, 1966, with the help of 2 Burmese brothers from Insein, namely, U Aye and U Soe Maung. I found my place among the first number on the roll.

I entered full-time service as an evangelist in December 1973, though I failed the Lord in a shaded interlude in 2001. I put my trust in His good hands and He fully restored me. My family and I moved to Munlai in 2003 and enjoy happy fellowship with the Church of God in Munlai.

BOB HAWTHORNE (England)

"Oh, when I look back now,
That summer seemed to last forever
And if I had the choice,
Yeah, I'd always wanna be there.
Those were the best days of my life."

Growing up in the 1960s, my teenage years were filled with music, football and various other challenges, and at the time they were very much 'the best days of my life.' But even then there were the questions that a lot of folk ask about life and death, like 'Where does God fit into it all?' I had gone to Sunday school as did many others, but it was whilst on holiday at my aunt and uncle's on the south coast that I was handed a leaflet with the statement: 'How to be saved.'

In very simple terms I was presented with the fact that because of sin (wrongdoing) in my life, even as a teenager, that any potential relationship with God was broken; but there was a way for restoration. The leaflet presented me with several Bible verses:

"For the wages of sin is death, but the free gift of God is eternal life in Christ Jesus our Lord" (Romans 6:23);

"For God so loved the world that He gave His One and only Son, that whoever believes in Him shall not perish but have eternal life" (John 3:16);

"If you confess with your mouth, 'Jesus is Lord', and believe in your heart

that God raised Him from the dead, you will be saved" (Romans 10:9).

Through the reading of the leaflet I realised that as far as a Holy God was concerned, I was guilty of disobeying Him, but His Son Jesus Christ had been punished at Calvary for my disobedience and all I had to do was repent and confess "Jesus is Lord." On the reverse of the leaflet there was a prayer, and as I said it, I knew that my life had been changed. Salvation was only through Jesus Christ who had died for me on the cross of Calvary, rose again from the dead, and gloriously defeated death, Satan and sin. Not long after I returned home, I met a Christian lady who invited me to church. A couple of years later I was baptised and became a member of my local church of God. The best years of my life? No – they have followed on through God's grace and kindness. I am indeed the most blessed of men.

JOHAN & ROSEMARY VAN HEERDEN (Federation of Rhodesia & Nyasaland, and Canada)

I was born in Africa. I grew up in the British colony known as the Federation of Rhodesia & Nyasaland (now 3 separate nations: Zimbabwe, Zambia & Malawi). My mother and father were not Christians. Father was an alcoholic; my brother and I coped as best we could in a dysfunctional family. One day, a day of which my brother and I remind one another, the Lord Jesus spoke to our hearts. He quite literally called us 'out of the blue', i.e. totally unexpectedly. I had been exposed throughout childhood to the Word of God as it was so regularly presented as part of the school programme. I was blessed in growing up in a time when the reading of the Bible and prayer was a normal part of the school curriculum , and so the Spirit of God no doubt used this in my conversion. In prayer, we accepted Jesus as our Lord. The following Sunday we walked into a nearby Methodist church. I was 12 at the time. Through the hymns of Charles Wesley, I delighted in praising my Lord Jesus:

"He speaks, and, listening to His voice,
New life the dead receive;
The mourning, weary souls rejoice,
The childlike hearts believe."

I met Rosemary in 1969. She was a CUSO (Canadian University Service

Overseas) volunteer to Zambia. She was a practising Roman Catholic. Within 2 months I asked her to marry me; she agreed. Apparently, my regular church attendance excited her. In Zambia, then Canada, we attended both the Catholic and United Churches. In Canada I soon became disenchanted with the United Church and its lack of commitment to the Word of God, so I left it. Reasoning that at least the Catholic Church stands firm on its doctrine, I considered converting to Catholicism. God had other ideas.

In Dundas, Ontario, I taught 'World Religions' at Highland Secondary School. There I met Mary Beck, a secretary at the school. She asked me if I needed speakers for my unit on Christianity. 'Only if they are fundamentalists,' I replied. That was my criterion for speakers of all religions. It kept things clear and sincere for the students. Mary assured me of that. She sent me Bob Armstrong & Ed Neely. Over the years both of them had a profound impact on my students and guests, such as Rosemary. As for me, I learned more Biblical truths from them than in all my years in the Catholic and United Churches. Now, the more I attended the Catholic Church, the more convinced I became of the error of its beliefs and practices. During the Eucharist I would counter-pray, 'There is no longer any sacrifice for sin.'

Then, one glorious day, the Lord spoke to Rosemary's heart through a radio ministry by John MacArthur. His topic was 'The Battle for the Beginning'. Rose was struck by two points: (1) the Bible is the final, the ultimate authority on all matters of which it speaks; (2) the Bible's authority is undermined whenever it is subject to man's interpretation, be it Catholic or scientific. In other words, the Bible means what it says, and says what it means. Rose realised that it alone was God's word; and that the book of Genesis was foundational to understanding and trusting the rest of its contents. She said to me 'Get me out of the Catholic Church!', to which I replied, 'Where do we go?' Her reply: 'You should know.' I responded, 'All I know is that there is no 100% Bible-believing church anywhere.' We were in a dilemma. For the first time in our married life we prayed together as a couple, asking our

Father in heaven to lead us to a church where He wanted us to worship Him.

We visited various evangelical churches, but found them wanting. Rose then said, 'What about that church you visited 20 years ago?' I had indeed visited the Church of God in Dundas a few Sunday evenings. I told her the church there had long since folded, and that the one in Hamilton was too far away. Rose persisted. So I called Laurie Williams, who had taught at Highland and had been in the Church of God in Dundas. I asked him for directions and a hat needed for Rose, being aware of the church teaching about head-covering! Rose and I attended many 'Remembrances' ('Communion' as generally known elsewhere) as observers. We were intrigued. This was definitely biblical, but so different from what we knew. But why shouldn't it be? Worship is not to be as the world dictates. Yet, I was hesitant. Rose noticed and asked why. Well, to be frank, I now realised what God expected of me. Up to that point, I had been quite content to pay pastors and priests to pray for me and preach to me. God was now shaking me out of my complacency.

Soon after, we were baptised by immersion and Sunday, 21 July 2002 was a truly significant day in our lives. On that day we were 'added' to the Church of God in Hamilton and our walk with the Lord became more real, more meaningful, and more blessed. The years since then have been a spiritual blessing beyond all expectation for Rose and me. The message is clear, and I can use a well-known hymn to express it:

"When we walk with the Lord
In the light of His word,
What a glory He sheds on our way!
While we do His good will
He abides with us still,
And with all who will trust and obey."
(John H. Sammis)

JOHN HUNTER (Scotland)

My full name is John McRae Hunter. I was born at home on 11 December, 1938, the sixth child in a family that consisted of 6 girls and 6 boys. When I was 9 we moved from our 3-bedroom house in Clarkston, Airdrie, to a 4-bedroom house in Gartlea, Airdrie. At that time there were 11 of us. We attended the High Church in Airdrie where we had all been 'christened' and I was a member of the Boys Brigade.

I was also a member of the Orange Order Juveniles, a strongly Protestant youth organisation that held marches that were anti-Catholic. I left that as a result of being made to march round the hall on my own because I had arrived 2 minutes late for a parade, while they sang "Onward Christian Soldiers."

I joined the Sea Cadets at 13 years of age, where I met my best friend Michael. I was made quartermaster and was with the officer who stood at the gangway, which was several yards long. Coming toward us is what I could only describe as your typical 'Teddy Boy' of that time, a lad wearing long drainpipe trousers with his long, coiffed hair. He stopped attending after a while and I was asked by the commanding officer to see why. Michael told me that 2 other cadets were bullying him. I told him if he came back I would make sure it didn't happen again!

I was working in the Imperial Tube Works in a squad of 6 men, one of whom was in the same class at High School as me. His name was William Kinniburgh. He was about to be married to a girl from Coatbridge and someone asked him if she had a sister who could be introduced to me. To cut a long story short, I got an invitation to the wedding and met the sister, who was called Betty. Betty and I arranged to meet the next night. I discovered Betty was a Christian and her church was just up the road from the fountain which was our rendezvous for meeting. We would meet there on Sunday nights after she had been to the evening meeting. One night I could tell there was something wrong with Betty. She told me she had been 'spoken to' by one of the elders about going with a lad who was not in the church and she would not be able to marry him while she was a member and he wasn't.

I had already mentioned to her about me possibly coming along to church with her on a Sunday evening for the gospel service, so the next Sunday I went along and after the meeting we were invited out to Martin & Mattie Lawrie's home - Mattie was Betty's Sunday School teacher. I had been attending these evening meetings for a few months when Betty decided she was not sure about our relationship. For about 2 months we went our separate ways. I still continued to attend the meetings and the pair of us were invited out still to the Lawrie's for supper. Martin would escort both of us to the bus stop at the end of our visit.

It was during this time and me attending gospel meetings that a man called Willie Easton came to speak. He was from Clydebank. At the finish of the service he invited anyone who wished to speak to him to come down to the front. I did, and after our conversation I accepted Christ as my Saviour. We knelt in prayer and I thanked God. Later on I was baptised in the Partick company of the Church of God in Glasgow and then later added to the Church of God in Coatbridge.

Betty and I have been married for many years now in God's grace and He has blessed us with a family consisting of youngsters reaching down to great-grandchildren.

WELLINGTON AGBEBAKUN IMOUKHUEDE (Nigeria)

From Mark Imoukhuede (son of the above):

One lovely Thursday morning in August, 1992, the Almighty God displayed His wonderful work of grace when my Dad, Wellington Agbebakun Imoukhuede, was 'born again.' He was about 75 years old when this great event took place. The change was real and the difference was clear.

It all started when I was informed about his ill health. I rushed to his home where I met one of my sisters who was a Christian. She had come as a nurse to check his condition, discovering, as she told my father, the results showed he had high blood pressure which was not good for his diabetic condition. By this time, I was already talking to him about the consequences should matters get worse, *"It is appointed unto men* [and women] *once to die, and afterwards judgement"* (Hebrews 9:27). My sister then decided to sing a song about the love of God. My Dad was very attentive, then came the tears. This was quite unlike him. I just felt the power of the Holy Spirit there in that room where this drama was unfolding. Now empowered by the Holy Spirit, I went on to challenge him about the goodness and mercies of God in his life. 'What would you say to God when you leave this world?' I asked. 'Surely, you have no one to blame but yourself.'

I should say that my father had been an idolater and a witchdoctor; a leader of a secret cult. He was the power of darkness personified. For this reason many people who came in contact with him were in great fear. It is noteworthy to say that by this time some of his children had accepted Jesus Christ as their Saviour and Lord, over a period of 27 years. As believers in the Lord Jesus we prayed fervently for his conversion; sought to live out a Christian life he could be convicted by; and often, as opportunity arose, spoke to him of the love of God in salvation for sinners through Jesus Christ His only Son. This lovely day in August 1992 was another opportunity for us, his family, to tell again the gospel story. This was really 'D-Day.'

I was very sure of the Spirit's leading as I spoke to him of the need to give his life to Christ. He had heard the gospel many times. 'Yes,' he answered. I went further, asking him when he would take the step. To my amazement, he said, 'Today.' 'Why not now?' I pleaded. That was it. He knelt down with eyes closed and prayed to God asking for the forgiveness of his sins and that God should make him 'His child' like his other children. He knew that some of his children were saved. After this prayer I showed him passages of scripture to give him the assurance of salvation. To give evidence of his new life in Christ, he burnt up all the articles of his trade in the witchcraft business. He withdrew from the leadership of the secret cult and told the cult members, 'I am reborn' (see 2 Corinthians 5:17).

Tough days were ahead, but he knew the Lord was with him. Not long after, he was baptised as a believer in the Lord Jesus and brought into the Church of God in Surulere, Nigeria. He passed on to glory only two and a half years later. 'Amazing Grace' indeed.

The very worst of sinners are saved when they come to God in repentance and faith in the Lord Jesus (Acts 17:30; 20:21). If Wellington Agbebakun Imoukhuede could be saved, so can anyone who calls upon the name of the Lord (Romans 10:13).

RODRECK JAMES (Malawi)

I am a maize farmer from Solomon Village, Ntcheu, Malawi. I am 42 years old and married with 4 children. I am a sinner (we all are). I used to tell lies, use insulting words, mistreating others often. I know that sinners will go to hell, but to believe in God is all-important. I need to repent of my sins, and also accept Christ as Saviour, and seek to follow Him. This I have tried to do.

At a funeral conducted by the Church of God in my country on behalf of a child who died belonging to the family of Nastaz Zamoya, who was in the church, I heard the Word of God from John's gospel chapter 14. I realised that things on earth are temporary but things in heaven are eternal, and I desire to be in heaven one day, which is very far better – hence I decided to confess my sins to God on 26th November, 2007. The word convicted me and I went home, knelt down and prayed, asking God for forgiveness and He forgave me, and I asked Jesus to be my personal Saviour. Now I am saved eternally.

My desire now is to read my Bible as God has delivered me from the hand of the Devil and put me into the hands of Christ where I am receiving light. I went some place to work for 4 months where my employer never allowed me to go to church. Now I have been baptised and attend church regularly.

FRANK JENNER (Australia)

Frank Jenner lived in Sydney, Australia. He was a sailor addicted to gambling. In 1937, someone told him about the Lord Jesus Christ and asked him, ‘If you should die today, would you go to heaven or hell?” He believed on the Son of God and His death for sinners on the cross, and was saved from eternal punishment.

This so changed his life that he vowed to God he would aim to put his vital question to 10 people each day. Standing in George Street, Sydney, during his lunch hour, he offered a gospel leaflet to any who would accept it. He confronted them also with the question that had been put to him. He did this for many years. Someone estimated he must have spoken to more than 100,000 people. Years later, many from all over the world testified that it was Frank’s question that caused them to endeavour to find the answer by placing their trust in the Lord Jesus Christ as their personal Saviour. Many of them became missionaries and evangelists.

JOHN H JOHNSON (Scotland)

My father died when I was 12 years old. We had been in the Church of Scotland but shortly afterwards there was a change of minister who did not preach the gospel, and my mother took my brother Joe and me to Barnards Court Mission, where I still can recall a sermon preached by a Mr Logan. He used an illustration from the First World War, 1914 -1918. A signaller went into what was called, because of the danger, "No Man's Land", to join a broken cable. He was successful but was killed doing so. They erected a memorial to him which showed his hands joining that cable, with a one-word inscription underneath – "THROUGH". Mr Logan used this illustration to bring home to the audience the bravery of Jesus going to a place where no one ever wanted to go – the Cross of Calvary – where with one hand He, the Saviour, took God's hand, and with the other the hand of the believing sinner, thereby joining both, having broken through the barrier of sin.

A short time later my mother was persuaded to join the Church of God in Greenock and I found myself in the Sunday School. I went to the Churches of God Camp in Cummersdale and professed salvation in Christ rather than be questioned by two of the Camp leaders, Mr Cuthbertson and Mr Prasher. When I was about 14 years old a visitor came to the Sunday School and spoke on Isaiah 53:6, *"All we like sheep have gone astray; we have turned every one to his own way; and the Lord has laid on Him* [Jesus, the Messiah] *the iniquity of us all."*

He said we have all done wrong things (and I heartily agreed); that sheep scatter separately all over the hillside (I knew this was so from the experience of observing them), "going their own way" (I knew I had always gone in mine). God had punished Jesus for our/my sins. Did I see myself in the first 'all'? Yes, I did. Did I see myself in the second 'all'? Yes, I did - unquestionably. 'If you see yourself in the first, and also in the second all, then you are saved.' A day or so later, I said to my brother Joe, 'I'm saved! You better get saved as well!'

JO JOHNSON (Scotland)

I was born and brought up during the 1960s in the shipbuilding town of Greenock, on the west coast of Scotland. Both my parents were Christians, numbered with the Church of God in Greenock, meeting at the address of 'Cedar Hall', 5 Ardgowan Street. I am the eldest of 5 children – 3 brothers and a sister. As children we used to happily sit on Dad's knee while he told us a Bible story before we went to bed. No one could bring these stories to life for us the way he did! For example, when telling the story of Samson and the lion, we waited with bated breath for the bit where the lion jumped out from the side of the road. Dad would suddenly roar and rise up from the chair with us falling off his knees. What excitement! On Sunday mornings, when very young, we sat beside our parents on the wooden forms in the church hall when the church met each week to remember the Lord Jesus' death and resurrection. When we sing certain hymns, even today, it takes me back to those precious times. My parents often invited friends home for supper after the evening gospel service when we would have 'sing-songs', lively and interesting conversation, and hearty companionship.

Over the years I heard many gospel preachers. I was familiar with the message of salvation, 'the good news,' and its acceptance through believing faith in Jesus Christ. When I was 10 I went to the Auchenfoyle Camp in Kilmacolm, which was on a field that belonged to the Black farming family, and had been gifted to the Churches of God for summer youth work. We slept in old army tents – fine if the weather was dry; not so when it rained! After supper each night we had a goodnight talk, essentially a message from the Bible, before going to bed. Each night the 'gas mantles' in the so-called 'brick tent' – our all-purpose meeting room, dining room, and games room – had to be lit. I remember the hiss of the gas lamps and the thump, thump, thump, of the petrol generator, powering the light bulbs in the tents, as we sang camp hymns and listened to the message. The speakers told us of the love of God in sending His Son to die on the cross for each one of us, and our urgent need to make matters right with God by trusting the Lord Jesus Christ as our own personal Saviour. At the end of the goodnight meeting, we were invited to stay behind for a chat, if so desired. I always avoided this and made my escape to my tent.

Although I had always believed all I had been taught from the Bible, there was an internal conflict going on – was I saved? Had I trusted in the Lord Jesus as my Saviour? Where was I going to spend eternity? For 2 years I put off the decision. At the age of 12, having heard different preachers speak about the return of the Lord Jesus to the air, even though hearing about it before, I began to think more of it. I believe the Spirit of God was working with me. Two of my brothers were saved already. If the Lord returned today, they would go to be with Him, and I would be left. One night, lying awake in bed worrying about all this, I said to myself 'This is silly! I know how to get saved. I know the text John 3:16: *"For God so loved the world, that He gave His only begotten Son, that whosoever believes on Him should not perish, but have everlasting life."* Why don't I do it right now?' So, I turned over on my pillow and accepted Jesus as my Saviour. I can't remember the exact words I prayed; I simply remember the peace that flooded my heart. I got out of bed, went through the kitchen and told Mum & Dad, who were thrilled to hear of my decision for salvation.

I started to read my Bible regularly. In time I came to the story of the Ethiopian 'Chancellor of the Exchequer', a eunuch. In Acts chapter 8, I read his statement "*Behold, here is water, what hinders me from being baptised?*" The words leapt out at me. I said to myself, 'There's a baptismal tank in Cedar Hall - what's to stop me from being baptised?' John 13:15 was also on my mind, *"If you love Me, you will keep my commandments.*" I resolved to take the matter further, which I did the following Sunday, approaching one of the elders in the church. He arranged, with a fellow-elder, to come and visit me with my Dad's agreement. Not long after this, I was baptised at the hall and the following week was added to the Church of God in Greenock. I count it the highest honour to serve the Lord in His house and hope that I can continue to do so until faith gives way to sight.

"*One thing have I asked of the Lord, that will I seek after; that I may dwell in the house of the Lord all the days of my life, to behold the beauty of the Lord, and to enquire in His temple*" (Psalm 27:4).

ALF KEATES (England)

Two essential facts: I was born in England in August 1923. I was born-again in Scotland in 1953. At 29 I moved to Scotland to work in the Burgh Surveyor's office in Coatbridge. As I had served 4 years in the RAF in the Second World War, I had only lived in my home town 25 years. Having lived in Scotland since 1952 I am still told, 'You don't come from round here'! At home as a boy, I was sent to Sunday School long before I attended day school. I was in the church choir for 4 years, hearing 2 sermons every Sunday, but never knowingly heard the gospel.

During my RAF service, I was stationed in Iceland for 4 months. I got to know the padre and found him interesting. He was an Oxford graduate in English Literature and inspired me to read the classics. We had a good camp library and there was an English bookshop in the capital. He did not preach the gospel, but then I didn't know what the gospel was, except one of 4 New Testament books. I told him I had never been confirmed in the Church of England. He made arrangements for my confirmation when I returned to the UK. I received notification to attend a service in a country church in Oxfordshire , to be confirmed by the Bishop of Oxford. I felt very out of place at 22 in RAF uniform alongside a dozen 12-year-old children! At the time, I thought this is the day which will change my life; but it was to be another 8 years before I began my new life as a Christian.

A year after moving to Scotland my wife and I visited my sister-in-law Annie and her husband Willie Stewart. He invited me for a walk in the park during which we had a long conversation. Until that day we had been only engaged in small talk. Willie asked, 'Do you believe in

Jesus Christ'? 'Yes,' I replied, 'I have always believed.' Willie wasn't satisfied with my glib response. He explained 'You have believed *about* him as you believed about Guy Fawkes, but you need to believe *in* him, believing in Him as your own personal Saviour, the one who died for your sins on the cross.' Eventually, I saw the truth of this and my life was transformed. It began with my first prayer as a believer, thanking God for giving his Son to die for my sins, and thanking the Lord Jesus for giving me eternal life.

My new life led in a new direction. I was willing to be a follower of Christ and took the next step of baptism, then being added to a church of God. My colleagues at work wanted to know why I didn't do the things I used to do such as the football pools, and vice versa. I was now immersed in local church activities in my spare time. Two young colleagues were so interested in the discussions about Christ that a year later they became Christians. One came into our church. They both later on in their careers became senior local authority officers.

I followed the progress of my old padre who became chaplain to Her Majesty the Queen at St. George's Chapel, Windsor. I wrote to him a few years after my conversion and thanked him for his help during our time in Iceland. I had looked through some of his books in the Mitchell Library in Glasgow, and wrote asking him why there was no reference for the need to accept Christ as one's personal Saviour. He did reply and thanked me for getting in touch, but gave no answer to my question about being saved.

JOHN KERR (Scotland)

I am very appreciative of the fact that I was brought up in a Christian family and had a mother who prayed for me. There is no doubt this contributed to my becoming a Christian while in my teens. It was not long before I realised that I seemed to be in the minority with my friends and had to put up with criticism and ridicule. This was intensified by the fact that unbelievers said I became a believer simply because my parents had told me, and I wanted to please them. As I got older, people claimed I did not know enough at such an early age.

So, firstly, I thought about what actually happened when I got 'saved' (as believing on Jesus as Saviour is called). The experience is very clear in my mind to this day. I was on holiday at a youth camp and this old man spoke to me about Jesus and God. He showed me from the Bible that I was a sinner in God's eyes and that Jesus had taken the punishment due to me when He died on the cross. This was God's way of making me acceptable to Himself, if I believed on Jesus as my Saviour. Clearly it was a matter of faith, and at the time I can say it was a definite spiritual experience which brought to me an assurance of peace with God. The problem later on was that I could not prove to anyone else the validity of the experience, or in fact that God even existed. At this point in my life as I got older, it became increasingly important to satisfy my mind that what I was believing was in fact credible, although it needed faith.

Bit by bit I discovered how credible it was to believe and also that many clever people also believed as I did. This was important, as I was able to show others it was more reasonable to believe than to be an unbeliever. The quotes from the Bible that guided me to salvation through faith in Christ as my Saviour are found in John 3:36, *"He who believes in the Son has everlasting life; he who does not believe the Son shall not see life, but the wrath of God abides on him,"* and Romans 10:9: *"If you confess with your mouth the Lord Jesus, and believe in you heart that God has raised Him from the dead, you will be saved."*

TONY APPIAH KUBI (Ghana)

It all started in 1986 when I travelled from my home country Ghana to Nigeria to find 'greener pastures.' I stayed with a friend in a suburb of Lagos, the capital city. During these years I was a member of the Roman Catholic Church, although I did not know the way of salvation. I realised there is a great difference between going to church and accepting Christ as Lord and personal Saviour. In all my years till then I just did what worldly people do and called myself a Christian. Life went on as normal until 1988 when my wife joined me in Nigeria from Ghana. My wife was a nurse by profession and sought employment, and we needed new accommodation as there was no room to live together where I was with my friends. One of her patients offered us accommodation in Surulere in a street called Falolu Street. In this same street was a church called the Church of God.

One Sunday evening in June 1990, while awaiting my wife returning from afternoon duty, I was standing at the front door and heard the preaching of this church through the public address system. I became interested in the message spoken by the preacher and later went to the hall and listened to the message which touched my heart deeply, and I accepted Christ. From that day I saw the beauty of God in my life and also the truth of baptism and God's house where I should serve Him. It was amazing grace that saved a wretch like me, and keeps me in His service.

W. J. LENNOX (Northern Ireland)

My father was a man of the world who loved his children and did his best for them in material things, but my mother, in addition to her full share of the burden of a large family, had the greater responsibility for their eternal welfare on her heart. Although brought up an Episcopalian she was led to the Saviour in tender years amongst the Moravians, and though quite clear herself that her children could neither be made 'members of Christ,' nor have their 'ingrafting into Christ signified and sealed' by baptism (so-called), she allowed it to be performed to satisfy her husband. It wasn't that father was much concerned about spiritual things, but he was proud of his own and his ancestral connection with the so-called Church.

Mother's early influence and teaching, followed by that of enlightened Christians after I left home, were blessed to me, and I was awakened to see the necessity for a vital change in my life. I felt the loneliness of distance from God. I knew that I was a sinner and if the matter between God and myself was not soon set right, I was in serious trouble. I tried to do all that I could by my own efforts in order to secure peace and rest, but no matter what I did my best yielded nothing. I was exposed and condemned to judgement. Then the Lord spoke to me very specially through Isaiah 53:6 - "*All we like sheep have gone astray; we have turned every one to his own way; and the LORD hath laid on Him* [i.e. His Son] *the iniquity of us all.*" My difficulty had been that I could not be sure Christ died for me. At last I saw that if I could see myself in the first 'all' (where I really did see myself) then why could I not see myself in the second 'all', and accept God's testimony that my iniquity was laid on and dealt with by Christ? This scripture, combined with Hebrews 8:12 – *"For I will be merciful to their iniquities, and their sins will I remember no more"* (which I read again and again) gave me full assurance of salvation.

The further part of my story traces the good hand of my God in leading me to find joy in His "good, and acceptable and perfect will" for His own redeemed people. I was baptised in a little 'Exclusive' meeting though differed from them in what they held as 'Household Baptism,' holding that none but believers should be baptised. I attended Presbyterian services, but having learned that God has not arranged for one man to take charge of a congregation, I could not continue there.

I also went to the Episcopal Church but neither Presbyterian nor Episcopalian insisted on the necessity of the new birth or the distinction made in Scripture between the regenerate and unregenerate, so I did not stay long. I then got in touch with Baptists and although no one was designated 'Pastor' it was one man who presided and directed the ministry, etc. At length I became aware of a movement among the meetings with which I had been associated for a time, 'Brethren', which gradually grew in strength, and was supported by a monthly paper called 'Needed Truth.'

This paper was devoted largely to the setting forth of the principles of the Church and Churches of God, the Fellowship, the Kingdom of God, the House of God, etc. It purposed to show from the Scriptures that God has arranged for a collective people on earth to serve Him until the end of the dispensation, and that those who claim to be disciples of the Lord should give effect to such principles, and thus know the blessedness of being in the will of God collectively, even though all believers may not so act.

The greater number of those in the meetings with which I was now identified did not like this line of teaching, and spoke of those who taught it orally or by writing, as carnal, legal, and without love etc., etc. I was confused as I could see a division taking place. At this point, a booklet entitled "The House of God" fell into my hands and it was a help to me. Previously I had no conception of a dwelling place for God on earth. I had desired to see souls saved, believers then being baptised and meeting together simply in the name of the Lord to break bread, and obtain comfort in spiritual things; but to have living stones built together to form a habitation for God had been a thing foreign to my mind. When pondering the matter at length and reading Exodus 15, the truth found in verses 13 & 15 came to me as light from God, and I rejoiced exceedingly at the idea of a habitation for God.

JENNIFER LITHGOW (Scotland)

I was born into a Christian family, having believing grandparents on both sides. You could say it was perfect; but, as in all lives, dark clouds would gather later in one's experience. I was brought up in the Church of Scotland until I was 7 years of age. Then my mother followed my aunt's example (she was a very godly lady), and after listening to Billy Graham, the American evangelist, preach on 'Pride', left the Church of Scotland and joined the Exclusive Brethren.

It was a puzzle to me that there was neither minister nor pulpit at the Brethren meetings. I wondered where the pulpit was. I concluded it must be behind the doors in the corner of their hall, but alas, 'No!' Every man in the church took it in turn to speak at meetings, which was very strange for a child used to the formal way of the Church of Scotland. But here I met my Saviour at 12 years of age. I heard of God's love for me as a sinner and I confessed my love for Jesus as my Saviour to my mother after a nervous young preacher had proclaimed the gospel. The text that convicted me was Romans 10:9. That night we sang, with others gathered, John Newton's hymn: "How sweet the name of Jesus sounds in a believer's ear." I was so happy.

Time passed, and at 14 I 'suffered' in the Exclusives. As a sect, they made people isolated from school friends: we were not to eat or socialise with them. My health suffered, and I lost a vital final year of schooling. I finally left the Exclusives at the age of 25 as their leader, Jim Taylor, proved corrupt. My family also left. We heard about a farm with 'Jesus Saves' painted on the side of the building. A friend from the sect was also looking for another church. He had been given a gospel leaflet by the owner of that very farm. Our friend's name was John, and he was a postman. The address on the leaflet led us to the Church of God in Methil. As a family we duly attended and then I saw from the Scriptures my need for baptism (Acts 2:41). I heard the Lord Jesus' call to "*Follow Me*" (John 21:22). I was baptised by full immersion and added to the Church of God in Methil, where I saw the scriptural pattern of serving God together with others. I was also struck by the knowledge these people had of their Bible.

That was well over 30 years ago now. By the grace of God I still worship in the Churches of God along with my husband, Ian.

GRANT LOCKSON (Malawi)

I was born on 14th October, 1982, in the village of Kamwiri T/A Njolomok in the Ntcheu District of Malawi. I was the second-born in a family of 2 children, a girl and a boy. My mother died in 1985. All of us attended the local Roman Catholic Church in the village. When I finished school after Standard 8 exams, I left home and arrived in the city of Blantyre as I lacked school fees to start Form 1. I was looking for a job, moving from place to place, office to office, house to house, but nobody would employ me without me providing certificates or references to prove I had finished school, or had been at least working somewhere else, and was trustworthy.

As I searched endlessly, I met other men who were 'in the same boat' as me. We talked about our problems and discussed how we might solve them. A company car of Eyeguard Security came and stopped where we were. A man came out and said he wanted men like us to work as security guards. We didn't hesitate, followed him to his office, and he gave us positions of work. Alas for me! The place was frequently looted by thieves. That same week they came and tied me up and took all the goods away. The owner took me to the police and I was kept in custody for 5 months without appearing in court, because there was no evidence against me. Eventually the police tired of keeping me in custody and took me to Chickiri Prison on remand. I was there for almost 7 months. Adding the 5 months already in police custody, came to a year without any court appearance to look at the case.

Life in prison was so very hard that at first I wanted to commit suicide. There I met a lot of people who had been in the criminal world a long time. Some were innocent like me, others illegal immigrants waiting to be deported back to their own countries. I learned a lot, though. Some prisoners do not change their behaviour when 'inside' and actually become worse. Others, normally innocent, do not want to see the inside of a prison again once they are released. We ate only once a day, then at 3:00 p.m. we were locked up for the rest of the day. From mid-afternoon we would sing 'spirituals' and Christian songs like 'Atlsogoleteni' and 'Packendo Woopsya.' Here we were, in the cells doing this, even though many were thugs. When arising the next day, I decided to join the 'born-again' group. They were in prison for other 'charges' as opposed to criminal ones. I also joined the prison school, given the name 'reform school' where inmates attend education classes. In that same year, some of us were sent to Zomba Prison to study for G.C.E. examinations, which I passed in 11 subjects, including Maths and English. I did my utmost to polish my performance in education.

It was at this time I was released and I turned my life around and gave it to Jesus. That was 7th July, 2004. Two years later on the 14th of the same month I saw people at the football ground, singing choruses and clapping hands. Some smiled as others were singing. They looked happy. These were the songs I heard that day:

"Amayenda ndi Yesi amaoneka (3 times this line is sung)
Amaoneka mayendedwe," meaning
'You can tell who walks with Jesus,
You can tell by the way he walks.'
and
"Amwayi oyenda ndi Yesu (twice)
Atsoka oyenda msatana" (twice), meaning
'Lucky are the ones who walk with Jesus (twice)
Unlucky are the ones who walk with Satan' (twice).

I stopped and listened. I decided to join them. When I reached the crowd some people laughed at me and wanted to get rid of me. Others said, 'Leave him alone, God has something for him.' It was true.

DAVID LUCK (England)

I was born into a Christian family but soon discovered this did not automatically make me a Christian. To begin with, I found I had a temper which I could not control. This caused the most hurt to those I loved best. The guilt I felt after these awful outbursts was unbearable. Another thing was, that although the rest of the family loved going to 'chapel', as they called it, Sunday was the worst day of the week for me. Furthermore, I was troubled by the fact that I felt unmoved by the narrative of the crucifixion of Jesus; this despite the fact I wept bucket-loads over secular tearjerkers.

This all changed during a family holiday by the sea. A Christian Youth Camp was being held near the resort where we were staying. The organisers had hired the local school where they held 'Gospel Services.' The subject one day was 'Light' and the preacher began by saying that the centre of our affections, the heart, is by nature dark because of sin. This is what had troubled me in the past, and that evening it weighed heavily on me. He then drew our attention to the Lord Jesus Christ who said, "I am the light of the world" and who so wanted to come into our lives.

Then he said, 'If you are in a dark room with no windows, you only need to open the door and the light will come in and fill the room. This is what you need to do with the door of your heart. Let Jesus in, and light will fill your heart.' I repented of my sin, knew the Lord Jesus had died for my sins, and there and then accepted him as my personal Saviour. What a great difference He made to my life. He has been my guide and help ever since.

MALCOLM MACDONALD (Scotland)

It was 1947, a winter of very heavy snow, reaching a depth of 6 feet. I had been to church in the morning, then Sunday School in the early afternoon. My teacher was Willie Whitelaw, an ordinary fellow, but something he said from the Bible that day made me aware I was very far from perfect. Troubled in my heart, I went home and spoke to my mother, who was a Christian. My concern was that if I died I would not go where Jesus was. My mother took me upstairs and explained very simply what I needed was eternal life. 'How do I get it?' I asked. She read and explained John 3:16, saying that whoever believes Jesus Christ is the Son of God, and the only Saviour, would never perish but have eternal life. I began to see that I could be included in the 'whoever' and made the all-important decision to believe and accept Him into my life. That Sunday afternoon changed my life for ever.

I attended a Bible Camp in Renfrewshire with my two older brothers. Each of us had believed and now we wanted, on hearing of God's desire for our lives, to be baptised - mainly as a result of the text in Acts 2:41. The baptisms of all three of us took place in 1949. Soon afterwards I was added to the Church of God in Kirkintilloch.

I can readily testify to the grace of God which has 'kept' me for over 50 years. I can vouch that the desire to see and serve the Saviour is still as bright as ever.

WILLIAM McCUBBIN (Scotland)

It was Christmas Eve 1948 and I was sitting playing in front of a coal fire. I can't remember what made me ask the question of my mother who was working nearby – 'Mum, how do you get saved?' I do know that I would have heard the expression many times, for I had been raised in a Christian family and taken to church every time there was a service! In reply, mother quoted the words of John 3:16, well known to many as a favourite verse of the Bible. By the grace of God it made immediate sense to me, and right then I put my faith in the Lord Jesus Christ. At 13 I was baptised and added to a little local church, and the story of my Christian progress should have proceeded seamlessly from that point on – it didn't. At High School I was impressed by how many of the teachers' lives seemed exciting and sophisticated. One master in particular impressed me, A.B., who, legend had it, was the holder of the Military Cross. He had been wounded while serving in the Tank Corps in the Western Desert. People like that made me begin to feel that God really had little to offer, and I soon got to the stage where I decided that God and I would have to part company! I wanted a life that would be exciting and successful.

At Easter in the year of my 15th birthday, I was taken to Larkhall for a holiday with Granny. My parents were to come and collect me at the end of the holiday, but when they arrived, I immediately knew something was wrong. My mother broke the news to me that A.B. was dead. I had said goodbye to him only 2 weeks before, and he had been in good health and high spirits. Now he was in eternity.

I went to bed that night, curtains drawn in the 'set-in-bed' that was common in households in Scotland at that time, and broke my heart at the news. It struck me powerfully that no matter whoever you are and whatever you achieved, a time would come when everyone would leave life as it is here, and give an account to God. On the last occasion I had seen him, a drawing was pinned to his board of a crucified Christ, in preparation for the work he had been commissioned to sculpt. He would never do it now. I was wondering if he knew the Man on the cross as his Saviour. The direction of my life changed that night. I might make mistakes, but I would never go back again to the life I had been living. The new life I had in Christ was reinforced and strengthened by that experience. As I write this, a shepherd's tobacco pipe from the Dardanelles that belonged to A.B. and that was given to me as a memento, is pinned to a wall adjacent to my desk as a reminder of him. I don't really need it – I'll never forget A.B., but I keep it there to remind me that I too will pass on one day and see the Man who died to be my Saviour those 2 millennia ago. I do hope I'll see A.B. again.

JOHN McGLINCHEY (Scotland)

There are times when I ask myself, 'Why did God choose to save me?' Times when I look back at the hand of God reaching into my life and drawing me to His heart. As a young boy born in the Gorbals area of Glasgow (notorious at the time for its 'toughness') I knew little of Christian life. Surrounded by over-crowded poverty in a seriously violent area, I found myself in a home where alcohol abuse and gambling very often led to virtual 'open warfare' - fighting within the single-roomed flat. Police often had to settle family disputes. I grew up thinking this was normal family life.

At the age of 15 my father died. My mother was in prison and my brother and I were left to make our own way in life, often with nowhere to stay. Thankfully I had pals who would let me stay with them for short periods. Life became desperate when a gang came looking for me and my brother. I was on the streets with nowhere to live. One day I asked a man if he knew where I could find lodgings. He directed me to an Irish landlady, telling me, 'She is a Bible-thumper; but she is a good landlady.' As I was now an atheist it would not concern me. I was now 17 and desperate to settle down.

For the first time in my life I met a real committed Christian who spoke openly about a God who loved sinners. One day I remember saying clearly to her, 'I do not believe in God.' She answered, 'Yes, but God believes in you.' She was a skilled soul-winner as bit by bit she revealed to my soul that I was lost in sin, but God loved me and Jesus died for me. Romans 6:20-21 was read, "*When you were the servant of sin you were free from righteousness. What benefit had you in the things you are now ashamed of?"* I could not escape the piercing logic of this question. The next two verses in the chapter tell the difference when you come to know Christ as Saviour: *"But now being made free from sin, and become a servant of God, the benefit is holiness and everlasting life. For the wages of sin is death* [death with no escape]; *but the free gift of God is eternal life in Christ Jesus our Lord."*

I still had many questions, doubts, problems and uncertainties, but one thing I was sure of was that I was a sinner, yet God loved me. I prayed: 'God, if you will give me the strength, I will become a Christian.' I got off my knees and had no faith in myself. 'I'll never make it.' But God had entered my life. Now I belonged to Him. He has kept me until now and will for all eternity. I went on to be baptised and brought into the Church of God in Glasgow. The Bible came to be my companion and I enjoyed studying it. Sharing my faith in God's love with others is my greatest pleasure. For many years I have had the privilege of visiting Barlinnie Prison in Glasgow and bringing the joyful news of God's love to the men within, in the prayerful hope of seeing God's wonderful power changing lives from being *"servants of sin to servants of God"* (Romans 6:19-23).

KAREN McILFATRICK (Northern Ireland)

Even though my parents are neither Christians or church-goers, they sent me along to everything that was going on in my local Presbyterian church in Ireland. Growing up I certainly had an appreciation for God and what he had done for me through his Son; however, making a solid decision to take Christ as my Saviour was more than I was willing to do at the time. I struggled to accept that becoming a Christian would be admitting my non-Christian family would go to hell.

Battling with this, it was easier to just remain ignorant and get on with my life, dealing with the consequences when such a time came. At the age of 16 I became involved with the Church of God and it was there that a close friend challenged me about 'my situation with God.' I explained that, although it was something that had been preying on my mind I wasn't ready to make any decisions. Shortly after, I heard a gospel message in which the man speaking appealed to the audience to pinpoint exactly what was holding them back from making a decision to follow Christ.

At that moment, I realised that until I addressed the issue and made a choice, I wouldn't be able to change my parents' situation with God either. So, it was that night, near my 17th birthday, that I accepted Christ as my Saviour. As I learned more, I saw the next step was baptism by immersion in water as a witness to my heart-belief, and then 'addition' into the Churches of God following that.

ANDY McILREE (Scotland)

It's often been said that God has no grandchildren; but it's equally true that having Christian parents allows a family to be in the mainstream of hearing His word. So it was for me.

Being born in Glasgow in 1946, my first taste of Sunday School was sitting around a huge pictorial Bible in Willie McKee's class in Duke Street, Parkhead, listening to the lovely way he had of talking about his Saviour, Jesus Christ. By the age of 8 I was well aware of John 3:16 and it was through this verse that God spoke to me during a time when I was off school with a bout of appendicitis. In the same year, our family went to live in a different part of Glasgow which introduced me to Shiloh Hall in the Govan area of the city where Mr Gordon Hume was my Sunday School teacher. He was a great encourager with a real interest in the boys in his class, and I well remember rising to the bait of his promised 5 shillings cash payment for anyone who completed a year's Bible Searchings, which appeared as a competition in the monthly magazine for Sunday School children entitled 'Eagles' Wings.'

However, going to the church camp at Kilmacolm for the first time was an even bigger attraction, though I little expected the discovery I would make there. It was an entirely new experience meeting boys from different parts of the U.K. and Northern Ireland, with lots of games and a variety of Bible-based meetings. For some unknown reason, probably the attraction of a run in an old Riley car, I ended up going with some of the older boys to a prayer meeting in Caledonia Hall, Greenock, and it took no time until I noticed Bible texts hanging on the walls. I don't remember anything at all of the meetings, simply because one of the texts so gripped my attention. It was Ephesians 5:1: "*Be ye therefore followers of God, as dear children.*" I went back to camp convinced that God had told me to be baptised, having already believed on the Lord Jesus as my Saviour. The great night of baptism came on 21st January 1958 in Hayburn Hall, Partick, and once again I had no inkling of God's plans for me in that place.

Only a year or so later, I started to attend a Bible Class there and came under the careful teaching of beloved Norman Miller. He was one of God's gentlemen: an artist in his work, and also with the Word of God, so there was a remarkable similarity what he did in his studio and what he did in his studies of the Bible. Patiently, he led us through the teaching of the Tabernacle, God's dwelling-place on earth; the animal offerings and sacrifices on the altar of Israel, God's people; the Feasts of Jehovah throughout the Jewish calendar year; and a comparative study of the gospels. It was fairly heavy going for a lad of 13, but Norman promised that God would illuminate what notes we took in coming years. He was right.

When school gave way to work it also gave way to the world, and many distractions obscured my earlier appreciation of the call of God to His service. However, at a particular crossroads when I felt spiritual progress was unlikely, He graciously appealed to the foundation that dear Norman had laid, and began to show me that His call had more to it than I'd ever anticipated. During my early 20s, the call to full-time service for the Lord gradually dawned on my unsuspecting spirit, and His confirmations were varied, primarily from His word, but also through remarkable circumstances and the involvement of men such as John Thomson and Jack Ferguson.

In the Lord's goodness, I was commended to full-time service on 13th April, 1976, and now, some forty-odd years later, I am more than thankful for His promise in Mark 10:29-30: "*There is no man that has left house, or brothers, or sisters, or father, or mother, or wife, or children, or lands, for My sake, and for the gospel's sake, but he shall receive an hundredfold more now in this time, houses, and brothers, and sisters, and mothers, and children, and lands"* – all of which He has proven to be true in the homes and assemblies of His people in so many parts of the world.

LAURIE MARTINEK (Canada)

I grew up being taken to church every Sunday by my mother, learning there many of the teachings of Jesus Christ, as well as in my grade school. My lovely little faith waned though in my teen years as I missed a church service here and there, and then another and another, and eventually attended rarely, and then not at all.

A few more choices, and in my late 20s I was already divorced and a single mother. I called out to God and confessed that I'd made a mess of my life and couldn't even blame Him. I had done this to myself. God was so merciful to me. I had a few years to let my heart heal and then He so graciously brought a wonderful man (now my husband) into my life. Such a dramatic turnaround. Happily married, two more babies, a lovely home, everything I ever wanted. But still, I didn't seek Him. And I struggled in my role as a wife and mother, blaming everyone else for my troubles. I ran out of give and contemplated taking my own life.

In a quiet moment while at home alone, God convicted me of my sin. I knew I needed Him back in my life. A friend invited me to hear the pastor speak one Sunday; it just 'happened' to be a gospel message. With trembling heart and sweating palms, I bowed my head, telling God I was so sorry for turning from Him, and coming to Him now as a last resort. I asked Him to save me. I had no idea what to expect. He answered immediately and I quietly gasped and whispered, 'You're there!' Burdens gone, filled with peace, a sense of purpose, and a decades-old swearing habit all gone in an instant. Miracle of grace.

All praise is to God for that poignant first 'memorial stone' and all that has followed these 22 years; a new Bible, eyes opened to the truth, baptism, church addition, a blessed marriage and family, and ever so sweet fellowship with Jesus my Lord. *"I have been crucified with Christ; and it is no longer I who live, but Christ lives in me; and the life which I now live in the flesh I live by faith in the Son of God, who loved me and delivered Himself up for me"* (Galatians 2:20). 'Amen' and 'Amen.'

HAKUNA MATATA (Malawi)

When I heard the gospel I felt everything the preacher said was directed to me. I remembered how I had suffered in custody. I had no one to save me or speak up for me. The preacher spoke of how the Devil enslaves people and only Jesus can break the yoke and set them free. The gospel message was from the first book of Samuel chapter 9 verse 27 about the lost donkeys: *"As they were going down to the outskirts of the city, Samuel* [the prophet] *said to Saul, 'Tell the servant to go ahead of us, but you stand here awhile, that I may announce to you the word of God.'"* I was really touched by the message and I asked God for forgiveness for my sins. Fear and all the evil deeds I had carried in me were removed.

The Lord said to me, *"Come now, let us reason together, says the Lord: though your sins be as scarlet, they shall be as white as snow; though they be red like crimson, they shall be as wool"* (Isaiah 1:18). I cried to God to forgive me. I looked very foolish to others, no doubt. Most knew me, but I still cried before them. When everything was over, together with others who came forward for prayer, I was counselled on how to live this new Christian life. The people who were there preaching told me 4 things to do: (1) Pray all the time; (2) Read the Bible all the time; (3) Testify to my salvation; (4) Have fellowship with other Christians.

When once I received the Lord as my Saviour, I didn't go back to the church my Catholic parents attended. My life gradually started to change. It was hard for my parents and fellow choir members to notice this change. I started to preach to others. My message was to repent of sins and receive the Lord Jesus as Saviour.

Over time, I met someone on 4th October, 2002 by the name of

Maunde at a place called Ndirande. We discussed salvation. He gave me his testimony of saving grace; I gave him mine. He asked me to see an elder of the church he went to called Mr Ntambalika the next day. I had lengthy discussions with this man. Finally, he got me to visit the Church of God he was in on Sunday, 6th, before I departed to Ntcheu. At the church we had prayer meetings and Bible Study groups where we would also praise the Lord. A person was also there called Mr Nemi who promised to visit my home village at Ntcheu, but I didn't believe he and Mr Ntambalika would come, as it was too far away from Blantyre. But on one of the days of the next week I received a call from the two men to say they were coming and would meet me at Ntcheu Boma.

Now I have turned my house into a house of prayer for all nations , as written in Isaiah 56:7. I'm so thankful to the two brothers in the Lord for encouragement. We have prayer meetings and Bible study groups in my house. My favourite book is the Acts of the Apostles and I particularly enjoy the conversion of Saul of Tarsus, and his life of service. Today, nobody can cheat me. By the grace of God I am what I am, and His grace towards me was not in vain (see 1 Corinthians 15:10). I also thank Mr Mark Imoukhuede for coming to my home although it is far away for him, for assurance and encouragement. These men have uplifted my spiritual life.

DANNY MAWHINNEY (Northern Ireland)

I have attended 10 summer camps organised by the Churches of God: 6 in Northern Ireland and 4 at Kilmacolm in Scotland. Many camping experiences come readily to mind such as the time 3 friends of mine and I set out for a short walk after supper one evening. We managed to get hopelessly lost and the walk lasted several hours. On another occasion I was thrown into the 'burn' (stream) at Kilmacolm; the only reason being because I happened to be Irish! Great friendships were formed at these camps and you met all kinds of people from all parts of the United Kingdom, and sometimes from overseas.

There is, however, one camp I'll never forget – the one at Lough Fea in 1949. Why? Because at this camp I received the most wonderful gift of my life. Something I shall never lose - the gift of eternal life. Let me tell you what happened. At these camps we were told about our lost and sinful position before God and how sin had separated us from Him. But, we also heard about a wonderful friend, the Lord Jesus, God's son, who left the glories of heaven for the shameful death of Calvary – "the death of the cross." One of the evangelists at this camp, known to all the boys as 'Uncle Geoff,' pointed out to me the last verse of John, chapter 3 in the Bible, *"Whoever believes in the Son has eternal life; whoever does not obey the Son shall not see life, but the wrath of God remains on him."* How simple the words.

In a moment I took God at His word and simply believed and trusted what He said. I had eternal life because of the finished work of the Lord Jesus on Calvary's cross. For this reason, this was the camp I'll never forget!

JOHN MAWHINNEY (Northern Ireland)

My conversion on 29th September ,1930, in poetic form:

For ever and ever I'll always remember
The twenty-ninth day of the month of September,
For then I said 'Farewell' to sorrow and strife
And I a poor sinner passed from death unto life.
For long had God's Spirit been striving with me,
Seeking to warn me from judgement to flee,
Seeking so earnestly, seeking in vain,
Always rejected, yet seeking again.
At last I was roused from my sorrowful state,
And thought with alarm of my terrible fate,
Should I die in my sins, and to judgement be led,
At this all my peace and tranquility fled.
Conviction's dread arrows then started to fly,
And found me defenceless, no shelter had I.
My soul unprotected lay naked and bare
And soon I was plunged in the depths of despair.
The Scriptures in secret I started to read,
These made me more wretched revealing my need,
Each verse that I read only deepened my gloom,
Pointing me forward to judgement and doom.
Each day as it dawned brought an increase of fear,
Each hour as it passed brought eternity near,
Each tick of the clock seemed a funeral knell,
Announcing my soul drawing nearer to Hell.

In torment by day and in torment by night,
I feared in the darkness, I feared in the light,
I feared to go out, and I feared to come in,
I plunged misery's depths in conviction of sin.
Though great my distress I sought it to hide,
And told it to no one, so great was my pride.
MY pride nearly hindered being made whole,
And pride will cost many a sinner his soul.
At last I was broken, no more could I bear,
And I sent up to heaven a cry of despair,
And He who is merciful pitied my case,
And gave me compassion – how matchless His grace.
He drew out the arrow that lodged in my breast,
He whispered 'I pardon', granting me rest.
He said in His kindness, "Let there be light"
And I in my blindness, received then my sight.
Oh, not even in glory will I ever know,
How much that He suffered to pay what I owe,
So near condemnation, so near to be lost,
Sweet, sweet is salvation, but 'oh', what a cost!
I'm living no longer in torment and dread,
I have happiness, peace, and contentment instead.
There now dwells within me a comforting Guest,
There's nothing can harm me; forever I'm blessed.
Each day as it dawns, brings me nearer to Home,
Each hour I am waiting to hear Him say 'Come',
Each tick of the clock seems to whisper so true,
'Soon He is coming, and coming for you'.
Oh, friend, be you Protestant, Catholic, or Jew,
My story can also be your story too.
The Saviour of sinners will turn none away,
And you too can have your conversion today.

MARGARET MERCHANT (Scotland)

I was brought up in a Christian home and made a decision to follow Christ when I was 11 years old. Unremarkable as that sounds, that decision had a profound impact on my life. More importantly it affected my whole eternal future. So, how was I able to make such an important decision at such a young age?

Both my parents, as said, were believers in God, read the Bible regularly, and prayed. I didn't always appreciate being summoned from play to listen to the Bible being read, but gradually, as prayer and discussion were encouraged, I grew to understand more about God and the love He had for each one of us that made Him give His Son to die for us on the cross for our sins. I had to own the fact for myself. It was not enough that my parents were Christians – I had to become one in my own right. That part was the work of the Holy Spirit. I needed to understand there was a gap between me and God and only He could bridge that by my being sorry for the things I had done wrong in offending Him, and accepting the wonderful gift He was offering of eternal life (and so many other things I did not fully understand, and still don't).

Over a period of a year or so, I had been thinking a lot about this. In a way, I wasn't surprised when an elder in the church we were attending asked me, 'Are you a Christian, Margaret?' The question caught me completely off-guard, as I found myself stammering, 'I... don't ... know!' I certainly knew then that I wasn't. It came as no surprise when the elder spoke to me again about my need of salvation. I was now only too glad to take the step of faith, believing that God would keep His promise and give me eternal life. Immediately, I felt a weight of all the wrongs I had done being lifted, and was very relieved. You might think an 11-year-old wouldn't have a great deal to repent of, but the experience was very real to me.

In the years following, I sometimes felt that nothing much had changed and wondered if my experience was real, but I would now say that in my life God has worked quietly and gradually, changing me slowly into someone He can use to do His work. I am very grateful I can thank Him for all He has done for me.

GEORGE MILLAR (Scotland)

I was brought up in a very strict Christian home. My father and mother were in the Church of God in Greenock. At an early age my two sisters and I were taken to 'the meetings.' Sunday/Lord's Day was the first meeting – the Remembrance – starting at 11:00 a.m., followed by lunch in the hall, then 2-3 p.m. ministry. Home for a break, to grandparents' house for tea. Sunday School 5-6 p.m. As we got older we stayed on for the prayer meeting at 6:30; gospel meeting 7-8 p.m. At these meetings we heard about the Saviour of sinners and I thought I knew all the answers! It was during special meetings in the hall in July 1937 that I accepted the Lord Jesus as my Saviour.

I was baptised on my birthday (13/03/1938) and added to the church. After many ups and downs I got married in 1952 and moved to the church in Kirkintilloch, where I later was made a deacon of the church. I served a number of years in the Scottish Camp committee and these were the best years of my life. I made lifelong friendships in that service. One of the highlights was being asked to baptise Alistair and Lindsay Coomer. I'll never forget that experience, having to remember and quote each of their many middle names, and the leaking of my baptismal trousers!

Above all was the opportunity of pointing young men and women to the Saviour during and after the 'good-night' meetings – to God all praise and glory. The mention of Camp sends a thrill through my being. Over the years I have encountered many disappointments but I'm truly thankful that when I faltered I heard the Master say: "Will you also go away?" Thankfully my answer came: "Lord, to whom shall

I go? You have the words of eternal life."

My father died when I was 9 and I am now a sick old man of over 81, kept alive with pills and the help of my heavenly Father, awaiting His call to take me home, when all shall be righted there!

MARION MILLAR (Scotland)

I had the privilege of growing up in a loving Christian family. I accepted the Lord Jesus as my Saviour at a young age. I was baptised at the age of 13 and was added to the Church of God in Harthill. Although the assembly was small we had a large Sunday School. This meant I was able to be involved in Sunday School work from the age of 15. Sunday School work and youth work were roles I thoroughly enjoyed over many years.

I met my husband David when I was in my teens. He was in the Church of God in Kirkintilloch. This became my assembly after I was married. During our time in Kirkintilloch our son Richard was born. We were delighted to become parents but we soon learned that Richard had been born with a heart defect and would eventually require surgery to correct this. Such times of worry bring you closer to the Lord. Richard had his operation when he was 5 and all went well. We were thankful for this after the years of worry. We were also thankful for the birth of our two daughters to complete the family.

David began to show the first signs of kidney failure when in his early 40s and started dialysis in his mid-40s. After a short time on dialysis he was accepted onto the list for a kidney transplant. Once again we relied on prayer asking that a suitable donor would be found. I felt led to ask to be considered as a donor. I felt this was the Lord's will and I was even more sure of this when tests showed that I was a suitable match for David but his mum, his dad and his sister were not.

After 18 months the transplant operation went ahead. Neither of us had any doubts that this was in the Lord's plan for us. We were aware that many people were praying for us and the success of the operation. All went well with the surgery and we both seemed to be recovering well. I was able to go home after 6 days and 10 days after the operation David said he was already feeling much better than he had done in months. Sadly, 3 days later he had a heart attack and passed away.

Those were such difficult days for everyone since this was the last outcome we expected after so much prayer and hope. I believed that God's timing was perfect and that He would carry us through this time of loss and what lay ahead. We were overwhelmed by the messages of sympathy received and the love and prayer support that surrounded us. The verses that particularly helped me at that time were:

Isaiah 43:1-2: *"Fear not, for I have redeemed you; I have summoned you by name; you are mine. When you pass through the waters, I will be with you."*

Jeremiah 29:11: *"For I know the plans I have for you ... plans to prosper you and not to harm you, plans to give you hope and a future."*

Times of such sadness draw you closer to the God of all comfort. You realise that the strength to cope comes from the Lord. I also needed the Lord's help to comfort and support my three children through this time of sorrow and loss.

The year after David died I was diagnosed as having Multiple Sclerosis. MS affects people in such varied ways and progresses at different rates. The Lord has been kind to me in that my symptoms have progressed slowly meaning I can still lead a relatively normal life with a few restrictions. I don't know how things may change in the future but I know with assurance that my loving Father is faithful and gracious and that He will support me through whatever lies ahead.

Psalm 46:1: *"God is our refuge and strength, an ever-present help in trouble."*

HANA MITSINDE (Malawi)

As I write this, I am in my second last year of school. Jesus, I know, has set me free from my sins. I knew I was a sinner because I often fought with others, insulted friends, stole writing materials at school, and told lies. If we go on sinning we will eventually pay the penalty if we haven't come to God asking for forgiveness, and believing that Jesus bore the punishment that was due to us for our sins. How glad I am I have taken Jesus as my personal Saviour. When I was at home on my own one day in April 2008, I was reading the Bible verse Luke 5:32, where Jesus says, *"I am not come to call the righteous (that is, self-righteous) but sinners to repentance."* I was a sinner, no doubt, but He came for sinners like me and you. That was why I knelt down to confess my sins and ask for forgiveness. Although I am young I know it is the will of God that I should serve Him. In desiring to follow Him I have now been baptised, which is His command.

LIAN ZA NANG (Myanmar)

I am also known as James. I am now 60 years old. I was born into a Christian family. I attended Sunday School and right from the first year I was awarded prizes for obedience to my teachers, good character, and diligence in learning. I was satisfied with my achievements. But at 18 years of age I was still unsaved, yet I had a fear of being sent to hell as I realised that only believers on the Lord Jesus would be saved and those who did not believe would be 'lost' for ever. So, after wrestling with my trouble for 2 years I came to believe and have the assurance of salvation; that was in 1979. The scriptures that helped me were John 5:24 and 1 John 5:10.

In 1991 by God's grace I became a full-time servant of the Lord and am married to Cing Kaw Hau. We have 3 children: Mary, Joseph and Benjamin. We live in the house that adjoins the Church of God hall in Munlai, where we are so happy to serve the Lord and have His blessing.

THOMAS OBONDI (Kenya)

My full name is Thomas Matwetwe Obondi. I was born in 1983 and I am a teacher in education. Since a young age I was brought up in a Christian family under the care of the Roman Catholic church. In 1993 I was christened in that church after undergoing Catholic teachings. It was not until 2015, however, when I was on my way to church that I heard someone preaching through the public address system. I suddenly stopped to listen. The preacher was talking about 'Three Churches', which, he said, are as follows:

1. The Church of God, which follows the teachings of the Holy Bible.

2. The church of men, which follows the teachings of men and their traditions.

3. The church of Satan, which follows the teachings of the Devil.

I wondered to which church I belonged. This message pricked my heart and I remained restless. I desired to be in the Church of God. After a time, I googled on the internet using my phone for more information about Churches of God. I came across a form on the internet where I wrote a message to seek for help concerning the Church of God the following day. One of the elders of the Churches of God responded to my message. I couldn't believe my eyes because of joy. He referred me to brother Mark Imoukhuede who wrote back to me and wished to know exactly where I came from, and my contacts. After giving him the information, I got his call one evening on my way from school. We arranged where to meet at his place of stay in one of the hotels at Ogembo town (Framil) the following day. That night I kept on praying to God to help me in my meeting with His servants.

The following day I met Mark and he introduced me to his fellow-worker Tony Nemi. We prayed and shared the word of God. They then invited me to attend the Sunday church services at Benmark's - a place of worship, on Sunday, 12th July, 2015. I attended the church services and requested the two brothers to share the message of God with my family members as they had wanted to meet and hear them after I had informed them. Mark and Tony agreed and we walked home that afternoon. They shared with us the word of God from Acts 9 - it was all about the story of Saul's conversion, who resolved to take a new direction, and changed his name to Paul after encountering Christ. We also learned that if we confess our sins with our mouth the Lord Jesus, and believe in our heart that God raised him from the dead, we shall be saved (Romans 10:9). Therefore on that day of 12th July, 2015 I confessed my sins and resolved to take a new direction. That was the day I received salvation. That day, too, our dear friends promised to send us 3 vernacular Bibles, which we later received and greatly assist us to grow by the Holy Spirit's help. Since that day I have been in fellowship with other church members and with the help of brother Jorom Benmark and the teachings I always get from brothers Mark and Tony whenever they make visits to Kenya, I have been richly blessed. I thank God that I am now finished with the 1st and 2nd stages of the 7 pillars of the churches of God as seen in Acts 2:41-42. I was the happiest person on Saturday, 5th December, 2015 when I was baptised. Miraculously the hour that I received salvation was the same hour that I was baptised, because both events took place at 2:00 p.m. in the afternoon. I thank God for that. I believe He who has begun good work in me will bring it to perfection. It is our prayer that God may turn many to the faith and bring them to give glory and praise to Him. We long for the day when more Kenyans will be found in Churches of God.

RYAN O'HANLON (England)

Since I came to know the Lord Jesus as my Saviour back in 2005, I can say that God has worked wonders in my life. So many avenues have been opened up, for which I am grateful, and have to say that if I wasn't a Christian I think I would have been in serious trouble with the law. I was up to all sorts of bad things and was filling the gap in my life with drugs, alcohol and the like, basically everything that wasn't good for the human body. I was forever in trouble at school with the teachers because I was always cheeky and getting into fights. The power of God had changed my life completely.

I was introduced to the youth club in Birmingham by my cousin Sammy and I decided to go along to the Midlands Youth Camp run by the Churches of God. I was a pain in the neck and no doubt gave the leaders a hard time. I knew it was a Bible Camp but didn't go to learn about Jesus and the Bible; just to mess around with the people who went from Birmingham. While at the camp, we (the Birmingham lads) called ourselves 'the Brummy army' and had 'turf wars' with the Wembley lads. We came out worse than them. Like any other 13-year-old, I had an attitude problem and thought I should be the centre of attention, so didn't listen to any of the Bible talks because I didn't know any of the leaders who weren't from Birmingham. When someone was talking who came from Nottingham or Wembley etc. I just switched off, started fiddling with my thumbs and closed my ears. When Jules Gregory was talking, who is from Birmingham, I decided to see what he had to say because I knew and respected him. And that night it hit me, when I saw my name come up on the screen. I decided that Jesus died for me and that He wanted to be part of my life.

Maturing over the years, I came to realise that baptism was the next step forward. After a few conversations with John Boyce about the subject, in September 2007 I began to attend the services of the Church of God in Birmingham – the Remembrance and prayer and Bible study on a Tuesday evening, and also T4G in John Boyce's house. I also had plenty of conversations with Christian friends. I came to the conclusion that if I wanted to please God then I must go ahead and be baptised. That took place on 27th July, 2008 and I was accepted into the church on 3rd of August. I was thankful for being able to go to events such as Convention 242, Young Peoples' Meetings, Birmingham/Buxton Convention, YFR Rallies, only to name a few. I have made so many new friends, though have to say I have lost contact with near enough all my old ones. People mock me because I go to church, and I always try to bring God into every conversation.

ALEX OSBORNE (Scotland)

I was born in Partick, Glasgow in 1961 and lived in Castlebank Street (now the Clydeside Express Way). My mum was a French polisher by trade and my dad worked in the local power station at that time. By the age of seven I was going to two Sunday schools: one at the Salvation Army and the other at the Church of Scotland where Mum and Dad were married. I would often go to local church youth clubs along with my older and younger brother. Even though I was very young, I was impressed by the leaders that ran these clubs: the care, interest and time they took with young people. I also heard many Bible stories here for the first time. Although my parents weren't Christians or regular 'church goers,' they encouraged me to go along to various church events.

When I was nine years of age, because of redevelopment in the area we moved to Hayburn Street in Partick, into a tenement building just opposite Hayburn Hall, Church of God. I remember looking out of my bedroom window and seeing the people going into the building. The ladies had fancy hats and some of them arrived in cars. We didn't have a car, so I thought they were quite posh, so I fancied going there! My brothers and myself started going to the Sunday School. My Sunday school teacher was called Lizzie Logan, and the hall seemed packed with various classes of different age groups. At that time, it was the norm to attend a Sunday School.

In 1971, aged ten, my other brother David and myself were invited to go to Auchenfoyle Christian Youth Camp near Kilmacolm. I enjoyed this very much, being in the country and sleeping in tents for the first time. At camp I enjoyed crafts, games, talks, competitions and playing in the burn which ran through the site. Each morning and night we had a short Bible talk from different leaders. Although I had heard the Gospel many times over the years, I had never been asked to make a decision to accept Christ as my Saviour. After one of the morning classes I spoke to a couple of the Camp leaders, Neville Coomer and David Renfrew. We read John 3:16 and although I knew this verse off by heart, I never realized until then that Jesus died for *my* sins. So, on 12th July, 1971, I asked in simple faith for Jesus to be my Saviour and I thanked Him for dying on the cross for me and being punished for my sins.

It was at camp a few years later that I first thought about being baptized as I wanted to follow the Lord Jesus as a disciple. I was baptized at aged 15 in Hayburn Hall. Steve and Margaret Henderson, who attended there, were a great encouragement to me over the years and helped me to develop as a young Christian. They moved from Glasgow to Thurso when I was 16 years old.

After this I started going along to the Barrhead Class run by John Kerr. My younger brother Neil and myself would go along to John and Mary Kerr's home for tea and then to the gospel meeting. There were many young people around in Barrhead and Paisley churches at this time, so we had plenty of company and encouragement as young Christians.

Over the past 47 years since I was saved (having put my trust in the Lord Jesus as Saviour), God has been good. I'm happily married with 2 grown-up children who are both Christians. We are a very close family and enjoy serving the Lord together. There have been many challenges and troubles; however God has said, in 1 Peter 5:7, "*Cast all your cares on Him, for He cares for you.*" It also says for our encouragement, in John 16:33: *"So that in Me you may have peace. In this world you will have trouble. But take heart! I have overcome the world."*

I served as a camp leader for many years and am still involved and passionate about the work of Auchenfoyle camp in bringing young people to hear the good news of the gospel and encouraging young people in their Christian lives. It is important for people to make the right decisions as it says in John 6:68: *"To whom* [else] *shall we go? You have the words of eternal life."*

JAN PATON (Scotland)

"Jesus Christ cleanses us from all sin." 'Again, Jan, but slower this time,' I was told. Everybody in the packed Gospel Hall in Methil, Fife, clapped as I was lifted from the seat I'd had to stand on to be seen. It was the first time I had recited a verse from the Bible. Verses of the Bible got longer as I grew, and by the time I was 6 years old I knew many of them off by heart. 1 John 1:7; John 3:16; Romans 10:9, and many others I could quote. I enjoyed singing gospel hymns and Sunday School choruses; I thought I was going to heaven! My parents and sister were saved – surely I was too! One day my mother pointed out to me that we all have to make the decision by and for ourselves. There's no such thing as a 'family ticket' to heaven.

I must have been very quiet for the next few days. This was such a personal thing I had on my mind. I knew many Bible stories, but the one that came to me was about Paul and Silas, put into prison for speaking about Jesus – and they were singing in the cell! Suddenly, an earthquake took place and all the prisoners' chains fell off them. The jailor responsible for them was about to commit suicide, when he heard Paul say, "*Do yourself no harm: for we are all here.*" *"What must I do to be saved?"* he asked. "*Believe on the Lord Jesus and you will be saved*", came the answer. Like the jailor, I believed on the Lord Jesus, and I know I am saved.

JOAN RASPIN (England)

I've hesitated about writing my testimony as I'm one of those Christians who can't remember a particular moment or occasion when I came to know Jesus as my Saviour. Rather, it seems to have been a gradual process, perhaps over several years. I was brought up in a nominally Christian family, and encouraged to go to Sunday School in the Church of England, where, as Dad used to say, we were taught to be a good person and as a result 'get to heaven.' During the Second World War my father stood as a 'conscientious objector,' along with Eric Winstanley, with whom he'd worked in the church social club. They had no support from the clergy or most of their friends in this decision, and both were ordered to do agricultural work for a couple of years (in my father's case, not before he had been detained for 4 months at 'His Majesty's pleasure').

While working on the farms, both Eric and Dad met up with members of the Church of God who had been similarly appointed to farm-work. Conversations developed, leading to chats with Matt Sands, George Brookes, and Arthur Roberts at Maghull, resulting a year or two later in Eric and his wife Jenny, then my mother and father, coming to know the Lord as Saviour, followed by being baptised, and then added to the Church of God in St. Helens. I was then, of course, around 8/9 years of age - and I began to attend the Sunday School in the Church of God in St. Helens.

I must soon have learned the Biblical teaching of salvation by faith as I remember my 'old' C. of E. Sunday School teacher telling me of someone who had died, and saying that person was now in heaven, as he had been a good man. I didn't dare to contradict her, but I thought that wouldn't necessarily be the case, unless he had trusted in the Lord Jesus for salvation.

My first visit to the North West Summer Camp of the Churches of God was in 1949. I remember Mr John Drain, an evangelist, asking me if I was saved, and I had to say 'No.' Sometime during the next year or so, having read the texts in the church hall on many occasions when attending meetings, Romans 3:23 seemed to speak clearly to me, showing that I was one of the 'all' it mentioned, and that I needed salvation. I can't say that was my decision-time, but I do know that, by February 1952, I was assured I knew the Lord Jesus as personal Saviour, and while singing a hymn 'Trust and obey', after one of Mr Joe Bennison's sermons, I decided that was what I should do – obey the Lord's command to be baptised, as Jesus was Himself. So, on 8th March 1951 I was baptised in St. Helens' swimming baths.

I can't say life has been all 'plain sailing' since then, but looking back I can most definitely affirm *"Thus far, the Lord has helped me"* (1 Samuel 7:12). I am so grateful for the way God has blessed me and given me a place in His house. A lot of help in my spiritual life has been by meeting many good Christian friends at camps, week-ends, and young people's meetings, as well as regular church services. Now that I am retired it's a joy to be able to share in the Lord's work without the distractions of work-stress, and God willing, I trust that I shall be able to continue for a few more years yet.

MARY REID (Scotland)

I cannot remember a time when I did not believe in God. As a child I had always gone to Sunday School, ever since I can remember. It wasn't my fault that the family was very religious (far from it!!), but being part of a family of 5 children, it was somewhere for the kids to go on a Sunday. I remember a time when I went to 3 different churches in one day – the Church of Scotland in the morning; Church of God in the afternoon, and Sunshine Corner in the evening. The last I liked best as there were prizes for answering questions! One afternoon about the age of 10, I was in Mr Cameron's class at Hebron Hall, where the Church of God in Bathgate met. He was reading John chapter 3.

My friends and I messed about as usual, not really listening to what he was saying. Suddenly, he said, 'Mary, stand up and read this verse out loud!' It was John 3:16. Then he said, 'Instead of the words "world" and "whosoever", you say, Mary Parker, in their place.' I stood up and started to read as my classmates giggled. I remember it as if I couldn't hear my friends making a noise. I became aware of a real warm feeling inside me. He asked me, 'Do you believe, Mary, what you have just read, that God gave His only Son to die that Mary Parker should have everlasting life?' I replied immediately, 'Yes!' I did believe in my heart that God sent His son to die on the cross for me, and that if I believed this, I was saved forever, and one day I would go to heaven to be with Him forever.

Over the next few teenage years I attended the Bible Class at Hebron Hall and Mr Cameron often asked me if I was still sure I was saved. I would always assure him that I was. Late teens saw me attending church very few times as I wanted to go dancing with my friends on Sundays. About this time I met my future husband, Alex, and as young couples do we spent a lot of time together, and often discussed religion. I told him I believed in God and His Son, Jesus, and that one day I would be going to heaven. I wasn't really well-enough read in the Bible to argue a case, and Alex wasn't sure if there was a God at all. Some months later Alex was asked by a colleague at work if he believed in God. He told him he wasn't sure; then they had a long discussion about spiritual matters. During the conversation, the person told Alex the Lord Jesus was coming back to take all those who believed in Him to heaven. This was a revelation to Alex and he wanted to learn more about Jesus. We talked about it a lot. We decided we wanted to learn more together and hear more about the gospel story and the Lord's return.

Alex asked his colleague if we could come along to his church – a company of Open Brethren. However, he asked Alex if he wouldn't mind waiting a while as he wasn't attending church himself at the time due to a disagreement with some men in the church. It had been some time since I was at Hebron Hall but still suggested we should go along to a gospel meeting there as I knew a few people and remembered they were friendly and kind. We slipped into the back row just as the meeting started. I cannot remember who was taking the service, but it was just like coming home! After the meeting Herbert Cameron shook my hand vigorously and, with a tear in his eye, said how delighted he was to see me, and was this my young man? As he had always asked me every time I saw him in his shop, or on the street, he asked again, 'Do you still believe you are saved, Mary?' 'Yes,' I said, 'but I have a lot to learn.'

We returned the next Sunday and have never looked back since. That was September 1967, a few months before we were engaged. We attended regularly on Sunday evenings over the next couple of years, learning about the Lord and what He had to say to us from His word. Herbert and others in the church were very helpful and kind, taking us to special meetings, baptisms, conferences etc. We waited until after we were married before we applied for baptism. Following that we were welcomed into and became part of the Church of God in Bathgate; that was April 1970. We continued in the church there for 8 years, during which time the Lord blessed us with 2 lovely children. In April 1982 we moved to England because of Alex's job and were numbered with the saints in Bolton until the assembly closed; then moved to the Church of God in Leigh.

I hope and pray that as long as I live, I will never stop thanking the Lord for the day when He chose me to stand up in Sunday School and, with simple childlike faith, accept His offer of salvation, and for giving His Son to die that I might live eternally. 'Thank you, Lord Jesus.'

FERGUS REILLY (Scotland)

I was born in Glasgow on Hogmanay, 1960. My parents, grandmother and aunt attended a small mission hall-style of church in Parkhead called 'The Church of God,' one of four in the city. There were many others in different places I had never heard of before. I went to the Sunday School there from an early age and enjoyed the singing and stories from my teachers Willie McKee and Fred Harvey. As a prize at one point, I received an illustrated Bible with coloured pictures which brought some of the characters in the stories to life. Jonah was always a favourite. I liked running and could relate easily to him running away, or trying to, from God. It was pointed out to me that God in His love didn't want people running *from* Him but *to* Him. What was I afraid of? Having my sins forgiven had great appeal, but how did you do it? Romans 10:9 was read and discussed, then I said a simple prayer and received the Lord Jesus into my heart as Saviour.

Shortly after, at the age of about 11, we moved as a family to Edinburgh. New home, new church, new school. These days you would automatically get counselling for such a cultural upheaval. There were a lot of young people my own age in the church there, some baptised as young believers and in the church, others not. I couldn't differentiate between their behaviour and my own. This, plus the death of my father when I was 15, held me back spiritually, but eventually about 10 years later I knew exactly what was expected and decided to get baptised and follow the Lord in my life as a disciple.

I hear many interesting testimonies these days of people being delivered from decades of drug and alcohol abuse, which is great, but that is not where I have been. I have to acknowledge the guidance and preserving care of God over the decades in between then and now, in married life, church life, business life and now into retirement. My testimony is 'Jesus led me all the way,' and continues to do so day by day.

ALISTAIR RENFREW (Scotland)

My parents were Christians who worshipped in the Church of God in Clydebank. As children we attended meetings there and often evangelists would visit and hold meetings throughout the week, as well as at weekends. We lived about 15 minutes from the hall and one night we had a visit from two evangelists, Guy Jarvie and Willie Stewart. At the end of the meeting we were invited to stay behind for a 'talk' about salvation. Netta, my sister, and I did so. Guy spoke with me, but I was struggling to accept Christ as my Saviour. Guy realised this, put his hand in his pocket, then said to me, 'If I gave you this pen, what would you say?' I replied 'Thank you.' Guy then said, 'That is all you have to say to God for sending His Son to die for you.' Immediately, I took Jesus into my heart. Willie Stewart spoke to Netta and the same happened to her. We both made our way home. Doreen, another sister, and David my brother, as well as Mum & Dad, were overjoyed to hear the good news. Not long after this we were bombed out of our house. We had to stay and sleep on the hillside at Duntocher for 3 days and nights, having taken our blankets with us, and not much else. Jimmy Barr from Galston came to seek us out and took us all to live with his family for over a year. We then moved to our grandmother's house until our Clydebank one was repaired. Netta and myself were later baptised in the hall in Paisley and joined the Churches of God.

PAULINE RENFREW (England)

I was born and brought up in the north east of England. In early days I remember bedtime as something special. My father used to tell us Bible stories and my mother would sing 'Safe in the arms of Jesus' before she put out the light. My sister and I were in separate rooms because we used to squabble if together; but I was never afraid of being alone.

My conversion was a very simple and private affair. I was 9 years old and we were on holiday, visiting my grandmother in Scotland. For some reason I woke up in the middle of the night, and for the first time in my life I knew I wasn't 'saved.' I was puzzled. I remembered a verse in the Bible (I now know it was Acts 16:31, which states *"Believe in the Lord Jesus and you will be saved"*). I felt I did believe in Him, but there was still something missing. How long I lay there I don't know, but obviously the Holy Spirit was working in me. I then realised I had never asked God to take my sins away. A very simple prayer followed, along the lines of, 'Please, God, take my sins away.' The result was instant peace and I went straight back to sleep. I knew something significant had happened to me. The next morning, I found a piece of paper, wrote my name on it, the date and the statement, 'I was saved here.' I then hid it in a book in my uncle's bookcase.

At the age of 10 I went to Church Camp for the first time, and heard about being baptised. Other girls were talking about it, and I just thought it was something I should do. I have never regretted the early commitment I made to follow the Lord Jesus. I now live in London. I teach Biology in a small college to 16–18-year-old students. I am not married (I have struggled with that) but at each stage of my career I have sought to find out from the Lord what His will was for me. He has led me to some very interesting places, including New Zealand, Belgium and Poland. I have more personal contacts than I can keep up with! The greatest joy of all is seeing people turn to the Lord for salvation in the simple way I did.

However, we must also be prepared to nurture those we bring into the spiritual kingdom; so I have a large family to look after! The fields are "white unto harvest" out there in our communities, even in the spiritual vacuum of materialistic Britain. We need to learn to go out to others, build up relationships with non-Christians, share their problems and have the courage to believe God will answer our prayers. Let us learn to work with other Christians too, so that we have opportunity to tell them the truth of Churches of God. We are not to lose sight of our primary call to *"Go, and make disciples of all nations"* (Matthew 28:19). I woke early today and began to sing:

"To be in Your presence, to sit at Your feet,
Where Your love surrounds me, and makes me complete.
This is my desire. O Lord, this is my desire."
(Noel Richards)

It's a lovely song. It makes me feel good. I know that I am in the right place.

DAVID RICHARDSON (Scotland)

I was born of parents who were both saved by the grace and mercy of God through faith in the risen and glorified Lord Jesus Christ. They had been baptised and were 'on the roll' of the Church of God in Glasgow, which in scripture is defined as *"the church of the living God, the pillar and ground of the truth"* (1 Timothy 3:15). My father told me Bible stories at bedtime, and answered any questions I had. The one thing that puzzled me was, with him being 'saved', why could he not save me?' He read to me the words written in Psalm 49:7, *"None can by any means redeem his brother, nor give to God a ransom for him."* He then explained this, saying only God can save you. I did not understand and was very disappointed. I did not tell Dad that.

When I was 10 years old I listened to a full-time preacher (evangelist) called Guy Jarvie who came to speak at the hall. He stated that Christ voluntarily permitted the human race to nail Him hands and feet to a cross that had been made from a tree, and everyone who is hanged upon a tree is accursed. In order that God could forgive our sins, even mine, He put them on His beloved Son who became the bearer of our sins. As God the Father is of purer eyes than to even look upon sin, because He abhors it, so He had to turn His eyes away from His beloved Son when He was being punished for our sins on the cross. The Bible says when the Lord Jesus was bearing God's judgement, which should have fallen upon us, the sun withheld its light and darkness covered the earth for 3 hours (Matthew 27:45).

Such was the depth of Christ's suffering for us. When on the cross still the Saviour said, "*It is finished*," the work of salvation, for us to believe, was fully done. He did that for you and for me. My sins are all forgiven, through Christ's sacrifice, and I have eternal life through faith in the *"Son of God who loved me, and gave Himself up for me"* (Galatians 2:20).

LEONARD ROSS (Scotland)

I guess it was a keen interest in cars that led a young 12-year-old, on Thursday, 14th July 1955, to have a look at the Auchenfoyle Camp Leader's car parked just alongside the cookhouse in those days (and it was a Jaguar, even more appealing!), little realising that this would lead to a conversation with him which would, in turn, lead to taking the first steps on the Christian path – a path which in hindsight I now see as one which the Lord had already marked out for my life, in His grace, and in which there would be a very close involvement with that same Camp Leader who was soon to lead me to Christ, and subsequently become my boss, father-in-law, fellow-elder, prayer partner, and mentor in every sense of the word; a man in whose steps I would follow in spiritual service within the Churches of God.

That afternoon he was having a brief siesta, and became aware of a face peering into the car and admiring the interior, and all the instruments on the dashboard. This led to a conversation and the Bible at hand being opened to Romans 10 verse 9, and the subsequent work of the Spirit of God enlightening a young mind, the prayer of acceptance of Christ as Saviour – long before known within his family, but never really personally accepted. The very real sense of happiness and joy that filled that young lad's heart as he ran down the concrete path to his tent is an emotional experience which has never left him all these subsequent years!

Going back to Camp year on year, and standing on that same spot where the car was then parked still fills me with a real sense of gratitude to the Lord – and my camp leader – for all that transpired that day, and in the years that followed. The following year at the same place, in another conversation with the same leader – this time in that little room then just adjacent to the dining hall – the matter of living as a disciple of the Lord Jesus was broached, and the need of baptism identified from the Scriptures, which he wrote down on a scrap of paper (treasured to this day!) led to being baptised as a 13-year-old in Hayburn Hall, Glasgow, on Friday, 21st September 1956 along with five or six others, and added to the Churches of God (Partick company) on the Lord's Day, 23rd September.

The move to Aberdeen in 1964 to be involved in the family business re-united us, and led to the process, with his encouragement, of a developing Christian experience: those morning prayer times before the business day began were invaluable, as was his teaching and companionship in the years that followed until his home-call in 1997. The words of Hebrews 13:7 continue to resonate powerfully: *"Remember those who rule over you, who have spoken the word of God to you, whose faith follow, considering the outcome of their conduct."*

SELLINA SAIZI (Malawi)

My father was a Muslim at first because his parents were also of that religion, but he gave his life to Jesus Christ before he married my mother. Now, because my father knew the truth of salvation he was also helped of the Lord to lead us to a Christian life.

Since early days, I was taken to the church of Seventh Day Adventists, where there was a class for young children. Our teacher was called Mr Demawa. He taught us who God is, who Jesus is, and also what Jesus had done for us. When I went home and asked Dad & Mum questions, they said what I had heard was true – "*Whoever believes on the Lord Jesus Christ will be saved for all eternity.*" I was a child of 9 at that time. Though now 'saved' I had much to learn. I was looking for the place that God wanted me to be to serve Him. When I heard of the Church of God in Blantyre, I went along and my heart was happy. I want to stay in the House of God all my life because it is where I find the truth of God practised.

ELSIE SANDS (Isle of Man)

My childhood with my parents and sister Linda was happy and active. We had fun, being without pressure for educational results. We were taught Scripture and heard many biblical discussions in homes of Christian friends. Music was a feature with much singing of choruses and hymns, especially when going on an outing in the car. We had no television, and were not allowed to go to cinema, dances, or pubs. We never had any thought that we were missing out by not going to such places. College and summer jobs broadened my horizons. It was a good thing I went to a mixed school!

My salvation experience took place when I was 8. It is still vivid in my mind. Though so young, I knew I was a sinner. I also had a fear of the dark. Dad told me that Jesus could help me with so many fears I might come across in life, but He must be in my heart. I needed to confess my sins, repent of them, and ask Jesus to come into my life. This I did one evening in the bathroom of my home. On my way to bed I had to test this out. Dark bedroom doorways frightened me, and as I went upstairs I paused at first. There was fear. My heart skipped a beat. Instead of running back down the stairs I asked Jesus to take the fear away. It went. It never came back.

At 14 I was baptised by Matt Sands of Liverpool in the Victoria Street Baths in Douglas, Isle of Man. His daughters Eppie and Sylvia were there too. From 1962 – 1964 I found myself in Liverpool and lived with a couple called Jim and Doreen Seddon while I studied at Liverpool College of Art. Circumstances then took me to Manchester where the Lord provided me with accommodation near the hall belonging to the

Church of God in Liverpool. I was involved with assembly activities for 8 years, and commenced my teaching career in Art. While helping a man called Bill Sands who was an invalid, I started a friendship with his son Colin. After 7 years we married, moving to London where Colin was studying. After a further 7 years I left teaching to have my son, Bill. We then moved to Groombridge where I had a daughter, whom we called Emily. When she was 10 months of age Colin my husband left the home. I was unprepared for this and totally cast myself on the Lord. No parents near either. I did not understand the situation that had developed.

In spite of it all, on reflection, many rich experiences and deep friendships came our way. The Lord was with me, I knew. Scriptures became alive and were available for the troubles others were going through. At this time I was painting calendars for assembly use. I became a dog-minder on people's holidays, staying in their houses at times. I asked the Lord to introduce me to old people in the village who needed help. I wish I had the time to tell how the Lord answered that prayer. Mary Weston and I did painted furniture, but scripture discussion and prayer times were the highlight. Bill was baptised while we lived there. Time came to be near Mum & Dad at the close of their lives. We went to the Isle of Man, letting our house back home to rent one in the Isle of Man. We became involved in the Sunday School there. Then I needed an operation for breast cancer. I had a wonderful experience with a verse very much in mind, *"Perfect love casts out fear."*

Dad became ill, went into hospital, and soon passed away. We then moved to be with mother. She lasted a year after Dad's death. The assembly had to close and mother died a week after that happened. We were transferred to the Church of God in Liverpool and sold our house in Groombridge. Bill went to study architecture at Oxford, and now lives and works in London. Emily, through various traumas, studied Art at Liverpool where she was baptised and added to the church. She met and married Zeb Williamson and they now live with their family in Trinidad, Colorado. My future is in God's plans and hands.

SAUL OF TARSUS (Turkey) - later known as the Apostle Paul

As recorded in Acts 26:4-5, 9-23:

My manner of life from my youth, which was spent from the beginning among my own nation at Jerusalem, all the Jews know. They knew me from the first, if they were willing to testify, that according to their strictest sect of our religion I lived a Pharisee. Indeed, I myself thought to do many things contrary to the name of Jesus of Nazareth. This also I did in Jerusalem, and many of the saints I shut up in prison, having received authority from the chief priests; and when they were put to death I cast my vote against them. And I punished them often in every synagogue and compelled them to blaspheme; and being exceedingly raged against them, I persecuted them even to foreign cities.

While thus occupied, as I journeyed to Damascus with authority and commission from the chief priests, at midday along the road I saw a light from heaven, brighter than the sun, shining around me and those who journeyed with me. And when we had all fallen to the ground, I heard a voice speaking to me and saying in the Hebrew language, 'Saul, Saul, why are you persecuting Me? It is hard for you to kick against the goads.' So, I said, 'Who are you, Lord?' And He said, 'I am Jesus, whom you are persecuting. But rise and stand on your feet; for I have appeared to you for this purpose, to make you a minister and a witness both of the things which you have seen and of the things which I will yet reveal to you. I will deliver you from the Jewish people, as well as from the Gentiles, to whom I now send you, to open their eyes, in order to turn them from darkness to light, and from the power of Satan to God, that they may receive forgiveness of sins and an inheritance among those who are sanctified by faith in Me.'

I was not disobedient to the heavenly vision, but declared first to those in Damascus and in Jerusalem, and throughout all the region of Judea, and then to the Gentiles, that they should repent, turn to God, and do works befitting repentance. For these reasons the Jews seized me in the temple and tried to kill me. Therefore, having obtained help from God, to this day I stand, witnessing both to small and great, saying no other things than those which the prophets and Moses said would come – that the Christ would suffer, that He would be the first to rise from the dead, and would proclaim light to the Jewish people and to the Gentiles.

GERHARD SCHLEYER (Germany)

I was born in Berlin 7 years before Hitler came to power. My best friend lived next door. His Dad was a high-ranking Nazi officer. He persuaded me to join the Hitler Youth Movement when I was 10, by forging my mother's signature on the consent form. While at school, I got enthusiastically involved in all the activities of this militant nationalistic movement. Within it religion was despised. This suited me fine as it had not featured in my upbringing. I did not believe in the existence of God.

In 1939, while still at school, the Second World War broke out. I can vividly remember sheltering in the cellar of my parents' house, gripped with fear, as I heard bombs falling. Soon my turn came to be enlisted in the armed forces. After training in occupied France, I saw front line action in Holland. Having been hand-picked for a mission in 'no man's land,' one day a group of us returning from this mission were spotted by an enemy reconnaissance aircraft overhead. We were on open ground, with unfinished trenches, exposed.

Soon afterwards we came under fire. With the sound and smell of shells bursting all round us I was frantic with fear and clawed at the ground to escape death. Not many days before I had seen the bodies of 3 soldiers killed by a direct hit. My thoughts turned to God: the God I believed did not exist! 'Please, God, help me. Don't let me die here!' Then I cried, vowing never again to say there was no God. Soon the shelling stopped. I had not even been wounded. I was subsequently engaged in other hazardous war activities, resulting in my being awarded the 'Iron Cross.'

I was captured a fortnight before the war in Europe ended. I was brought over to Britain, ending up in a Prisoner of War Camp at Ayr in Scotland. I befriended a fellow-prisoner who was a Christian. He in turn had made the acquaintance of a member of the Church of God in Ayr. Between them, they got the idea of organising a meeting at the church to which all the P.O.W.'s from the camp were invited. The response was tremendous; the hall was filled; and the gospel preached. There was a snag, though. Most of the Germans could not speak or understand English. This was where my friend stepped in. He acted as an interpreter, his English being very good.

After this I attended more meetings, but the language was still a problem. My friend was aware of this, so one evening, walking 'home' to the camp, he spoke to me in my mother tongue. He told me of God's love for me, sending His only Son to die for me on a cruel cross, bearing the punishment due to me on account of my sins. All I needed to do was to believe it and accept the Lord Jesus into my heart. This I did, and know that one day I'll see my Saviour who loved me, and gave Himself up for me. The cross of Christ is God's way of salvation. Over 50 years later I am still following the Man who died on the cross for me.

"For all have sinned, and fall short of the glory of God" (Romans 3:23).

"To all who receive Him, He gives the right to become children of God, even to them that believe on His name" (John 1:12).

DOREEN SEDDON (England)

I grew up in a Christian home. My parents were very godly and found great joy in their Christian faith. They were so happy to find themselves in the Church of God in Liverpool. Our childhood was a very happy one. As with most people in this situation, it is very hard to 'escape' the gospel story, hearing it every week at Sunday School and the gospel meeting. When I was about 10 years of age, I became quite anxious that I wasn't 'saved.' My brother and sister had already put their trust in the Lord Jesus as their Saviour, and my brother had also been baptised after his conversion, and was in the church. Looking back it appears I must have been saved about half a dozen times, as each Sunday I would run home from Sunday School and kneel by my bed and thank Jesus for dying for me. I knew I was very bad as I had told lies at times and had recently stolen plums from outside a shop, and also apples from someone's apple tree.

Directly after I prayed, I would get up off my knees and look in the mirror to see if I looked any different, and thought I cannot really be saved because I can't cry, and a few people I knew who had been saved seemed to cry! One Sunday, my teacher asked me if I would like to tell the other girls in my class at Sunday School how I got saved. My heart raced as I was now having to own up that I wasn't sure if I was. Once I told her this, she pointed me to a text on the wall of the building which said, *"He who believes in the Son of God has everlasting life."* She then asked me if I did believe that Jesus died for me, and I said 'Yes.' She then said 'You must thank Him then.' My heart felt full of joy. God has said if I believe I have eternal life. I had got it. Shortly after that, I was baptised and added to the Church of God, but when I was 14 or 15 years old, my mother became very mentally ill and was hospitalised for 2 periods of 6 months in a mental hospital. During that time I really fell out with God, not being able to understand why He had allowed Mum to be so ill. I became very cross with Him.

I left school at 15 and went to work in an office, which I very much enjoyed. The time drew near for Mum to be discharged from hospital and my Dad was told she must not be left on her own. Dad was very worried that my brother was doing an apprenticeship and my sister was still at school. He felt I should give up my job to look after her. Life from then on was not easy. My mother who had been loving and caring became quite difficult to handle. I had a job getting her up and dressed. One morning when I was getting all steamed up and doing the washing, Frank Jones from the church came round to see how I was coping, and found me in tears. He said, 'I will speak to your Dad and see if you can come and work in my photography business, just in the mornings for a few hours.' I was so pleased. Things went well, but I still hated God for allowing my Mum to be so ill.

Church Camp time came round and Frank suggested I should go to the camp for the weekend, but I didn't want to go and came up with all sorts of excuses; however, the matter was overruled, and I did go. When Sunday evening came, I had my bag packed to go home but decided to sneak into the big marquee where Mr Prasher was telling the story of the Ethiopian Chancellor who listened to Philip the evangelist reading Isaiah 53:6: *"All we like sheep have gone astray ... and the Lord has laid on Him the iniquity of us all."* It was as if God was speaking directly to me. Yes, I was going my own way, and I had this wonderful Saviour – what on earth was I doing? The Ethiopian believed the scripture that it spoke of Christ, the Son of God, then asked to be baptised, and following that, he went on his way rejoicing: and here I was being so miserable! I had to leave to catch a bus and my heart overflowed with joy. I was thanking God for His goodness to me.

When I reached the station I started telling people on the platform about the wonderful time I had at the camp and how wonderful the Lord Jesus was. The next morning I went into work and Frank Jones asked me how I got on. I was bursting to tell everyone and one thing I do remember saying was that I had decided there was something wrong with people in the church. He said, 'Why?' I said because they all look so miserable. He said, 'Calm down, it will wear off.' But, do you know, it has never worn off. I have let the Lord down many a time, but He has always been there for me, helping me. The hymn is true: 'Jesus gets sweeter as the days go by.'

RUTH SEDDON (England)

My Family I am the eldest child of Christian parents, Harry & Joan, and have 3 brothers, Paul, Pete & Dave, and an extended family of sisters-in-law, Ali & Pam, plus wonderful nieces and nephews, Rhi, Ceri, Christopher, Helena and Michael. I truly give the Lord thanks for each and every one of them. There at the beginning of my life, till now, always ready to support, care and love me through all my highs and lows, in ways too numerous to count. I love them as a rich blessing from the Lord. No family is ever perfect, but for me mine comes pretty close! *"His* [God's] *faithfulness continues through all generations"* (Psalm 100:5).

My Faith Brought up in a Christian home I have no recollection of a clear time when I was saved, but I do remember when I was 10 years old at Billington Camp, a leader said, 'You're saved, aren't you, Ruth?' I said 'Yes... Less than a year later I was baptised and the only clear thought I have from that time was thinking I didn't want to be left alone in the back row in church, so I'd get baptised with Alison Webster. My teen years are a blur and my next spiritual milestone was when I reached 24. To cut a long heartache story short, I was definitely 'pulling angrily at the leash' about my Christianity and being in the Church of God, and thinking the grass is greener on the other side. However, the Lord was good to me. He loved me and gently *"drew me with lovingkindness"* (Jeremiah 31:3). I was at the lowest ebb of my life, yet my family kept loving me and the Lord channelled His kindness through one good friend who never gave up on me. I have never been as low since then. Job 34:29 says, *"When He gives quietness, who then can make trouble."* I feel if you've been brought up as a Christian and taken to church, there comes a time when faith is challenged and you need to decide how much Jesus means to you. In owning Him as Lord of my life then, and having Him as my best friend now, I can truly say He's never let me down and is always there for me.

My Friends Although I've never been blessed having one special person to share my life with, I am so very thankful He has given me so many other friends, both in and outside the church. I have also had time and opportunity to serve Him that I probably wouldn't have had otherwise – camps, youth groups, catering, giving talks, etc. My life is full and satisfying. Some years ago (another long story) I changed a wonderful job as a midwife to a clinical trainer and sales rep; I am travelling all over the country for days on end. It was all in God's plan, no doubt about that, yet I wondered why? I no longer have the opportunities to establish long-term relationships, nor to witness, feeling I have even less time than before. It is a lesson I am in the middle of learning. The Bible tells me/us: *"Be still, and know that I am God."* I see parts of His creation I have never seen before. I have more time to pray and listen. My life has never been busier with my family, my faith, and my friends. To cope I need, we all need, His inner peace: *"Let the peace of Christ rule in your hearts, and be thankful"* (Colossians 3:15); *"That we may truly have life and have it to the full"* (John 10:10).

ROBERT SHAW (Scotland)

I was blessed by being born into a Christian family, the younger of 2 children, my sister Lilian (called 'Lyn' for short) being two years older. My father, Robert, was the youngest of a family of 8 (4 boys & 4 girls). My paternal grandfather was a coal merchant from Falkirk, but lived most of his married life in the east end of Glasgow. He was called home to glory 8 years before I was born. I have always regretted not meeting him; several anecdotes suggest he was quite a character. For instance, to relieve a sore back caused by coal bag carrying, he would sometimes sleep on the concrete floor of the family kitchen. If he was unable to sleep he would sing – at the top of his ample voice – various hymns that he loved. He loved the Lord Jesus Christ and was an elder in the Church of God in Glasgow when the Fellowship of the Son of God, comprising churches of God worldwide, was formed towards the close of the 19th century. All my grandparents had been 'called home' before I was born.

My mother, youngest of a family of 3 (with 2 brothers) was brought up in the Parkhead area of Glasgow, adjacent to Celtic Park, the home of Glasgow Celtic Football Club. She attended a large Sunday School of about 300 children run by the Parkhead company of the Church of God in Glasgow, where she came across one of her cousins, Fred Harvey. His friend John Rae had brought him along. The two men featured prominently in the affairs of the church in the 20th century. Mother's parents were God-fearing but with no church allegiance. Her maiden name was Lily Mutch. In due course, both father and mother were saved, baptised and added to the Church of God. They married in 1930.

7 years later my sister was born. My birth coincided with the outbreak of the Second World War!

The war years impacted on my early life. Although very young, I was aware of danger and uncertainty as from time to time friendly helpers would arrive late at night to take mother, sister and me into underground shelters as a precaution against enemy aircraft. Father meantime was on a 'fire-watching' shift. As an engineer, he was engaged in producing marine instruments for ships. Several times, coming home from duties, he narrowly escaped death from shell and shrapnel.

Being committed Christians my parents took my sister and me regularly to church services and Sunday School. Neither Lilian or I complained about this, though none of our 'pals' were as 'committed to church' as we were! Dad was an elder in the church. We lived happily in a red sandstone tenement building in Dennistoun, Glasgow. We had 2 rooms, known as 'the kitchen' and 'the room.' Mum & Dad slept in the kitchen, Lilian and I in 'the room.' When we bedded down at night we had been taught the importance pf praying to God, thanking Him for what He gave us and asking for what we wanted to talk to Him about. Usually, father would be listening to our prayers which were spoken audibly. In July 1946 after prayers, and as we each said 'Goodnight' to him, Lilian suddenly said 'Dad, I got saved tonight.' He was overjoyed. He asked Lilian if I had heard her speak. Mum came through and expressed her delight at the news. I wasn't pleased at all, I was concerned - the reason being my father had told us of his younger days at a summer Christian Camp. One story was about a man called Dr Luxmoore who sometimes went round the tents at night as the boys were quietening down for sleep. He would pop his head through the laced-up tent door to say something that would make them think about Jesus. One night, in his rounds, he recited a short poem:

'My old companions, fare ye well,
I will not go with you to Hell;

I mean with Jesus Christ to dwell,
Will you go? Will you go?'

Apparently, it was a verse of an old hymn, but it sure was scary! Now, in the context of the home, it came to me with thumping clarity that my mother and father were saved, and talked often about that fact, but it had never registered with me that I, personally, had to be saved, even as a young boy of only 7 years of age. Now my sister was saved! I was the 'odd one out.' I realised that if Jesus came back again, as God's word promises, to take all those 'saved ones' to heaven, I would be left behind. I had been told He could return anytime.

Two weeks later, at supper, I asked father to explain John 3:16. I had heard this verse read and quoted so often as the way to obtain salvation. He did. Strangely, I don't recall ever doubting anything written in the Bible. I now knew I had to make a conscious, personal decision to trust for my salvation in Jesus Christ who died for me – as if for me alone. I made the decision, told my parents, and slept well that night, fully realising I was saved, 'not for the years of time alone, but for eternity.'

I had a bosom pal called Jack. We met at our church. We attended different schools as we lived a distance from each other, but both our fathers were committed Christians and often travelled together to different venues, so we were taken along with them. Other youngsters also were there. We also attended summer camp. On summer Saturday afternoons, with me not yet in teenage years, a number of church people met at different places in the country to distribute gospel literature. Jack and I would sometimes travel there on our bicycles. On one occasion, a kindly man from one of our churches caught up with me, put his hand on my shoulder, saying: *"I made haste and delayed not, to observe Thy commandments"* (Psalm 119:60). Then he walked on! I discovered subsequently he was a window cleaner.

Thinking about what happened, I realised that God had used Mr Stewart to encourage me to get to know God's commandments for His children and obey them. By this time I was 11 years old, but still timid and reserved. I needed a 'push' and got one! I got a second push when my sister asked me if I would like to be baptised since she wanted to take this step of discipleship. We both knew being baptised in water was the first step in obedience to the Master's will (see Acts 2:41; Matthew 28:19-20). Now it was to be a happy reality.

The baptism took place in August 1950 and we were added to the Church of God in Glasgow. We were the only disciples to be baptised by Mr Joe Galloway, who with his dear wife, some years later, was tragically killed by poisonous fumes from a faulty heating system. Sadly, my close friend Jack did not follow as a disciple.

God has blessed me with a hugely loving and supportive wife, who is also my best friend. Our two boys, Trevor and Lennie, love the Lord and are following Him, as their wives are too. We could fill pages with clear evidence of God's marvellous kindness. There have been times of leanness and fatness, materially and spiritually, but we rejoice in His mercy. Neither of us have a favourite verse but, like many others, we rejoice in the truth of Proverbs 3:1-10.

GRACE SHORE (England)

A young lady called Gill Mansfield, now with the married name Gill Toms, approached me with a rounders bat. She had come to Valentine's Park with a group of girls and saw me with some of my brothers, and invited me to play with her and her friends. My brothers departed quickly. When the time came for them to go back to the home of Mr A. G. Jarvis Snr., where they were having a girls' class, she asked me if I would like to come along. I returned home to ask my parents if that was alright as it was just round the corner from where I lived. They agreed to let me go. When I arrived I heard choruses being sung and the first one I learned was "At the cross, at the cross, where I first saw the light." The second was: "Living He loved me, dying He saved me." At the age of 12 I went to the South East Camp run by the Churches of God and heard more of what Jesus had done for me. I was asked about salvation, and I responded 'Yes, I am saved.' I haven't any exact time or Bible verse. I just simply believed the message of salvation when it was first told me, and also through reading the Bible and singing choruses at the girls' class, Sunday School and gospel meetings.

I started work at 15 years and then attended the weeknight meetings for prayer and teaching of God's word. The homes of the families in the church were always open to me and I was taken to Young Peoples' Meetings and Conferences at weekends. I wanted to be baptised but my parents refused as I had been christened, and on the form for that event the word 'baptism' appeared. There was going to be a baptism of another girl when I was 18 and I asked a gentleman named Hendy Taylor, who was now my Bible Class teacher, if he would speak to my parents to see if I could be baptised at the same time. After speaking to them for some time, with me making numerous cups of tea, they agreed, and so I was baptised and then came into the Church of God in Romford. The verse in the Bible that has always been precious to me is, *"Trust in the Lord with all your heart and lean not upon your own understanding, in all your ways acknowledge Him"* (Proverbs 3:5). My favourite hymn in the Gospel Hymnbook I have is:

"Where He may lead me, I will go,
For I have learned to trust Him so,
And I remember 'twas for me,
That He was slain on Calvary.
Jesus shall lead me, night and day,
Jesus shall lead me all the way;
He is the truest Friend to me,
For I remember Calvary."
(William Clark Martin)

DAVID SHORT (Scotland)

David was born in 6 August, 1918. He came from a family of strong medical and Christian tradition. His father Latimer was a public health physician, and his uncle, Arthur Rendle-Short, was professor of surgery at Bristol University. His 2 younger brothers also became doctors. Educated at Bristol Grammar School, he won a MacLoghlin scholarship of the Royal College of Surgeons to Clare College, Cambridge, where he graduated in 1942. He completed his clinical studies at Bristol Medical School, where he gained the gold medal.

After house officer posts at Bristol & Hampsted General Hospital, he decided that his pacifist viewpoint was no longer appropriate and joined the army medical corps as a lieutenant, later promoted to captain, serving in India and Burma from 1944–47. During the latter campaign he was in charge of a group of stretcher-bearers ferrying casualties from the front line to the field hospital. Feeling he was too far removed from the reality of war, he willingly entered into danger zones at the risk of his life.

Following demobilization, having already completed his M.D. during military service, he added a Ph.D with seminal research on pulmonary hypertension. His interest in cardiac research lasted throughout his career. He was a consultant by the age of 30 and some years later was appointed consultant physician in Aberdeen and started weekly post-graduate teaching in 1961. He also was responsible for commencing Christian services in Aberdeen hospitals. The physician to the Queen, Sir George Middleton, a GP in Ballater, consulted him on various health matters and in 1964 this led to him being asked to care for Prince

Charles when he was admitted with pneumonia to an Aberdeen Nursing Home. In 1977 he was appointed physician to the Queen in Scotland. Before retiring, he was given the post of Emeritus Professor of Clinical Medicine at the University of Aberdeen and chaired many high-level medical committees.

David was a committed Christian and was for many years an elder of an independent evangelical church, preaching regularly. He sought to integrate medicine with his Christian faith and, from 1964, as joint originator of weekly church services at Aberdeen Royal Infirmary and Woodend General Hospital, he was often seen propelling wheelchair-bound patients down corridors to services. He wrote books and papers on a variety of subjects. Always approachable, he had a deep sense of the equal value of all human beings before God and conversed easily with all levels of the social spectrum. Possibly thousands of Aberdeen students came for Sunday lunch to David & Joan's (also a doctor) house over the 45 years they lived in Aberdeen. At his church, he was frequently found sitting alongside any homeless people who came in to hear God's word being preached.

David faced his end with quiet assurance in the grace of God. He managed to combine in his life superb clinical skills, active research, compassion for his patients, and real interest and care for his staff. He was a wonderful role model and a great man. In stark contrast, his own estimate of himself is summed up by the epitaph he chose for his grave: 'A sinner saved by grace.'

SIR JAMES YOUNG SIMPSON (Scotland)

When I was a boy at school I saw a sight I shall never forget – a man tied to a cart and dragged before the townspeople's eyes through the streets of the town I lived in, his back torn and bleeding from the lashes of a whip. It was shameful punishment – for many offences? No, for one. Did any of the townsmen offer to alleviate his suffering? No! He who committed the offence had to bear the penalty alone. It was the penalty of a changing human law, for it was the last instance of its infliction. When I was a student at university, I saw another sight I can never forget – a man brought out to die. His arms were pinioned and his face was already as pale as death. Thousands of eager eyes were on him as he came up from the jail. He underwent the sentence of the law – for many offences? No, only one! He had stolen a money parcel from a stagecoach. He broke the law and died for it. It was the penalty of a changing human law in this case also. It was the last instance of capital punishment being inflicted for that offence. I saw another sight, it matters not when – myself a sinner standing on the brink of ruin, fully deserving nothing but God's judgement – for one sin? No, for many sins committed by me against the unchanging laws of God. I looked though, and saw Jesus as my substitute, scourged in my place, dying on a cross for me. I looked long and wept, and I was forgiven through His precious blood shed for me.

KARL SMITH (England)

I don't remember when I first believed in the Lord Jesus, but I do remember when I first *knew* I did. My parents believed in Him and used to send me to Sunday School, amongst other things. One week a well-known preacher was having special meetings for kids and had given out tiny little golden books with verses in them. I was looking at them in the hall of the church the Sunday afterwards, and one verse stood out. It said, *"God, have mercy on me, a sinner"* (Luke 18:13). I was only little. I wasn't a mugger or an axe-murderer. I hadn't even vandalised a telephone kiosk! But I knew I was what the Bible called 'a sinner,' even if only because sometimes I did the exact opposite of what my parents told me ... 'just *because.*' I also knew that God had mercy on me; that is, He wasn't going to punish me for my sins because He had punished the Lord Jesus instead when He was on the cross. I had personally trusted Him that He had done that, and that was enough as far as God was concerned.

It sometimes used to bother me that I didn't know exactly when I was 'born again,' but my Dad, knowing my simple childlike faith, asked me if I could remember the moment I was born. Of course, I couldn't. Then how do I know I had been? Because I was 'alive,' in the sense of being very aware of the place God had in my life. Well, I may not remember the exact moment, but I had the new life the Lord Jesus gives, and so I could know for a fact that I was born again. Didn't the Bible say that everyone who believes has everlasting life (see John 3:16)? I didn't doubt that I was saved for ever too much after that.

As I have grown up, the Lord has led me through the good and the bad times alike (there have been more good than bad for me so far). I have seen Him answering some very specific prayers and have been constantly aware of His love for me.

VERA SMITH (England)

I was 22 years old and married, and had been invited to a church camp for girls. Standing around the campfire one evening one of the younger girls said to me, 'Are you saved, Topsy?' (my hair was very curly in those days!). I looked at her and thought, 'What is she talking about? I never heard such a thing.' Suddenly there were a dozen pairs of eyes staring at me curiously and I felt myself blushing to the roots of my hair. I was so embarrassed to think this young person (to whom I shall be eternally grateful) knew something that I, at my age, didn't know. I very hesitantly replied, 'No, I don't think so'; but that question sent me off to someone who would enlighten me.

I found Mr John Drain, an evangelist with the Churches of God, who helped out as a spiritual leader at the camp, asking him what the young lady meant. He took me into the big marquee for quietness and privacy to speak, and for the first time I heard the true meaning of the death and resurrection of the Lord Jesus Christ. I also learned that I was a sinner and that it was for me He died, because He loved me and wanted me to repent of my sins, accept Him as my Saviour, and go to live one day with Him forever. As the Scriptures were being unfolded to me, I realised how much He had suffered on my account. I know that if I cut my finger it hurts, and when I think of the weals on His back; the raw flesh exposed like furrows in a field from the lashes of the soldiers' whips; the dreadful thorns piercing His head; His face bleeding where His beard was pulled off, I felt the guilty one; just as though I had taken the hammer and knocked those large nails into His hands and feet. It all became too much for me and the tears flowed freely.

In those days, the Girls' Camp ran for 2 weeks, so I returned the following week when I had an early leaving time from work before my day off. I was able to stay overnight at the camp. Later on the next day, a strange feeling came over me. I rushed out of the tent, and felt the need to hold on to something solid. There was a large tree nearby to which I rushed and threw my arms as far as I could round it. I felt that at any moment I could float away or faint. My monitor must have seen me, because she came to investigate. When she came to me and realised what had really happened, she wept tears of joy to hear that at 11:30 p.m. on the 30th July, 1947 I fully accepted Jesus Christ as my Saviour.

WILSON SNEDDON (Scotland)

I was born in Kirkintilloch, a few miles from the city of Glasgow. I had a fairly normal upbringing but had no interest in spiritual matters, even though my mother was a baptised believer and attended services at the local Gospel Hall. I know she prayed for me, and one of my earliest recollections is of her kneeling beside my father when he had come home drunk. She was praying that he would come to know the Lord Jesus as Saviour. Well, the day came when he did accept the Lord Jesus into his life; consequently I had my two parents now praying for me.

I enjoyed going about with my friends and we frequented the cinema and the gambling school, none of us with any thought of our spiritual state. One night at the cinema, I saw a film entitled 'Sign of the Cross' and watched as Christians were put to death because they believed on the Lord Jesus. I thought it strange that anyone would want to die for their faith. A few nights later, out with my friends and at a loose end, one of them said, 'Let's go to the Gospel Hall and amuse ourselves.' I answered, 'No, we can't go because my mother will be there.' We then decided to go to the little Church of God hall in Donaldson Street. That was the best thing I could have done, for there I heard about salvation. When the meeting was over, a man called Frank Docherty asked me if I would like to be saved through believing on Christ. I replied, 'Mister, I don't know how to be saved.' He sat down with me and my cousin and told us how easy it is - just believe on the Lord Jesus Christ as your Saviour. So I gave my life to the Lord Jesus Christ that very night.

When I got home I told my parents what had happened, and took a packet of cigarettes out of my pocket and threw them in the fire. I had a changed life. That took place on 29th November, 1946. I was later baptised in the same hall and can testify to the saving grace and keeping power of our Lord and Saviour, Jesus Christ.

BEN STRACHAN (England)

One night as a child I was sitting in the back of the family car being driven home from church. I remember thinking over what the speaker had said in his gospel message. God gave me faith that night to believe. I knew and accepted that this Man named Jesus who had been spoken about, had died for me on the cross because He truly loved me. In time, I came to understand and grasp hold of the fact that He was also God, and during His agonising death on the cross He had dealt with my sin, and because of His death I had been richly blessed with so many wonderful blessings. At the age of 19, having left home to study, I chose to be baptised and give my life over to seeking the things of God. One of the greatest of these is that through the Lord Jesus Christ and by the help of the Spirit of God I can, with other fellow-believers, bring worship and praise to His God and Father.

LIAN KHAW THAWNG (Myanmar)

Just before the Second World War a Christian preacher came to our village with the message that all people inevitably have to die, but those who believe in Jesus Christ shall rise again from the dead to live forever (John 11:25). I was 12 years of age at that time. The message sank deep into my soul. It is still living in me and will never go away from me. Praise God.

At 17 I met a Christian family in a neighbouring village and was in their company as often as I could be. Through them I came to realise that having believed on the Lord Jesus, I should follow Him in being baptised in water, which took place in 1959. I joined the Church of God in Khumnuai when it was planted in 1981. My joy is the same as when I first believed. Serving God in the small assembly and eagerly awaiting the return of the Lord Jesus to take all who believe in Him to be with Him for ever is something that thrills my heart.

ALAN TOMS (Wales)

I think I was about 10 or 11 years of age when I took Jesus as my Saviour. Sadly, I was too shy at the time to tell anyone about it. Had I told my mother she would have taken a note of it. Thankfully, I eventually got over my shyness.

I was born into a family where Christ was loved and we went twice to church on Sundays, so I knew plenty about the Lord Jesus, but didn't know him personally. The friends in church often spoke of the Lord's return to the air to receive and take away from this earth those who believed on Him. I knew that when He came, Mum and Dad would be caught up to meet Him, and be with Him for ever. This bothered me, for I knew I would be left behind. In fact, I was so troubled that one day I plucked up the courage to ask my grandfather how I could be saved. We were walking on a cliff top. I recall it vividly. He was man of few words, but told me enough to give the help I needed. 'Read John 3:16 and put your name in the verse,' he said. That night, kneeling by my bed, I went over the verse "*For God so loved the world*" time and again, 'and I'm in the world and of the world,' I reasoned, 'so He must love me.' I followed through the other words of the verse inserting my name. I'm sure that was the night when my name was written in heaven. I guess I missed out somewhat on the joy of it, and perhaps even the full assurance, by not telling someone; but that came later.

A year or so later, I was fortunate to have a Sunday School teacher who was great with boys. Fred Ollis was his name and he was a greengrocer. He had a little corner shop selling fruit and vegetables. One Sunday afternoon he was reading and commenting on Isaiah 53:5-6. He asked the group of us when we got home to write it out on paper, putting our own names in the verses, similar to what my grandfather said to me with John 3:16. We gave him the cards back, and years later he informed me that he still treasured those bits of paper with Isaiah 53:56 on them. I treasured the assurance, once again, that little exercise gave me.

My story doesn't end there. Romans 10:9 says, *"If you shall confess with your mouth Jesus as Lord, and believe in your heart that God raised Him from the dead, you shall be saved."* In my childlike understanding, Jesus was Lord when I first believed. Now I knew I must live to please Him. With growing knowledge, I understood His Lordship demanded continuing obedience. At 14 years of age I was baptised and came into the Church of God in Cardiff, my hometown. Looking back over the years, I thank God for the privilege of serving Him.

BRIAN TUGWELL (Wales)

My mother was a regular at the local 'Brethren' church in Tiverton, Devon. In the quietness of a midweek prayer meeting she gave her heart to the Lord Jesus. Presumably, she heard something in a prayer that drew her to the Saviour who died for her. My father had some Sunday School attendance behind him when he joined the Navy during the early days of the war. He had wanted to be a fighter pilot but his eyesight was not up to the required standards. He was regularly witnessed to and attended a Brethren church in Bristol. The Saviour found him and Dad hauled his colours to the mast by declaring God's love for him. My mother was posted to Bristol to work in an armament factory and attended the same church as my father. They were soon courting and married in 1945 when the war ended.

Some years later, my folks moved to Cardiff. After witnessing at work one day 2 believers made themselves known to him. They both belonged to the Churches of God, a group similar to 'Brethren' but with clearer defined unity and held together by a united elderhood. The latter was a new truth to my parents and they grasped it fully. Soon, Thelma Stockwell and Martin Follett, Dad's new Christian colleagues, invited him to their meeting place and not long after Mum and Dad were added to Churches of God. Christ was no stranger to our home. He lived with us and hugely affected all we did as a family. My father felt it wrong to catch a bus on a Sunday as that meant someone had to work on that special day for God. We therefore walked the 4 miles there and the 4 miles back to church. If Dad went twice on a Sunday, we tramped 16 miles. Whether my Dad was right or wrong, I had no idea at that stage of my life. What it did show me was that he held fast to his convictions and the Lord and His will were important.

One summer, my brother attended camp and must have come back fired up for he proceeded to ask me if I was saved. Such terminology was not understood by me and I must have muttered something incoherently. My mother had large ears and having overheard the chat called me to the kitchen. Carefully explaining that God loved sinners, but not their sin, she reminded me that Jesus came to die for me. This I was acquainted with but did not know I needed to be saved from the penalty of sin. She suggested I might like to go and talk to God about it. I did, kneeling by my bed, and saying, 'I believe in you, Jesus. Thank you for dying for me. Please take away my sins.' I went to the kitchen with tears streaming down my face. 'What's up?' asked Mum. 'I don't know if I said it right.' Her wise answer was 'The Lord understands what we mean.'

So that's how I got saved. I don't think I knew until years later that was the moment I turned from darkness to light, or understood the term 'born again.' Yet, I do know that was the time my eternal salvation was clinched and guaranteed. Over the years, I have learned how merciful God is to save someone with a heart as wicked as any other. The great cry should ever be, *"God, be merciful to me a sinner,"* for *"Whoever calls on the name of the Lord shall be saved."*

GERARD DE VOS (Belgium)

I was brought up a Roman Catholic and christened as a child. While at school, we were regularly taken to church, and during that time I received my 'first communion.' By the time I reached 20 or so, I realised I had no relationship with God. I would have described myself as a believer even then though, but I knew there was something missing in my life. There was something more that I didn't have. However, the sense of emptiness became less acute, and I settled into a nominal belief, in which, by some vague way, I felt God wasn't far away. For a while though, I searched in wrong directions, such as Jehovah's Witnesses.

Then, thanks to Charles Van Der Weehe, I came into contact with a full-time worker with the Churches of God named Brian Johnston. At last I understood the gospel and came to know the teaching of the Churches of God, as summarized in the '7 Steps' of Acts 2:41-42. That sense of missing out on something, the emptiness, the vagueness in my belief, was now gone. I am so glad to be a 'born-again Christian.'

MARGARET WEIR (Scotland)

My parents were Christian, as were my maternal and paternal grand-parents, so there was a strong Christian influence in my life from an early age. I don't have a Bible verse or time or date to pinpoint when I first believed on the Lord Jesus as my Saviour, but I can remember thinking about Him when I was around 6 or 7. As I lay in bed one night, a graphic picture came into my mind of Jesus on the cross. I wept quietly as I contemplated His suffering by crucifixion. The following day I forgot all about it, but at night again the scene came before me, this time less vivid. From that time I never doubted that He had died on Calvary for me.

As a child I liked to hear Bible stories and for a time I attended 3 Sunday Schools. On Friday nights I also went to Children's Meetings at a local mission. These were happy occasions and very popular with kids. One night, I think I would be 10 at the time, an invitation was given for anyone who wanted to be sure about salvation to wait behind; so I stayed. The people assisting at these meetings were caring and kind but some lacked counselling skills. One woman, without any conversation with me, passed me to another lady with the words, 'She's not saved!' She probably reached that conclusion because I was quite small. The person who sat with me was no help at all and I became a bit upset and eventually went home. That night, in the comfort of my bed, I went over in my mind again and again that it didn't matter what that woman said, I knew I believed on the Lord Jesus. That may have been the night I became a Christian.

As a teenager I didn't have any companions or opportunity to attend

Christian gatherings. When I turned 22 I went to Canada for a few years and quickly became good friends with a Christian girl at work. I also made other Christian friends. I read my Bible and knew I should be baptised but was reluctant to make any further commitment or change aspects of my life, although increasingly I was more comfortable in Christian company. After baptism, wishing to please the Lord Jesus in my life, I had some regret that I had made my decision more because I felt it was right, rather than out of love for Jesus. Later on I learned from verses like John 14:21 that God looked on a person following the teaching of the Lord Jesus as an expression of loving Him.

STANFORD WEZALAMU (Malawi)

I grow maize and cassava on my farm in Changa Village, near Ntcheu. I was a drinker and a smoker, but stopped these habits a few years ago. I discovered I ran short of money most times in my home and business life and this was leading me to poverty.

I 'stumbled' into discovering the Church of God. I had been attending a church called 'Abraham Church' from 1977 - 2005. I left because there was no difference in lifestyle between those who were in the church and those who were in the world. In the Church of God I found a great difference. After these things, I just stayed at home, not going to any church for 3 years, although in my heart I was still searching for the right place to worship. The Spirit of God impressed on me to start going to church. I heard the Word of God at a funeral service in February 2008 at the age of 50.

The message was from John 14:1, where Jesus says, "*Let not your hearts be troubled. Believe in God; believe also in Me.*" The verse urged me to believe in God and Christ. I was also convicted of my being a sinner who needed repentance. I had been committing adultery. The consequences of my sins were too fearful to think about, but through believing on Jesus as my Saviour I came to know freedom and forgiveness. I knelt down and prayed, knowing God had forgiven me that day and gives eternal life to all who put their trust in Jesus as Saviour.

I have observed great changes since I was brought to Christ; one being a new appetite to read the Bible. Although baptised by immersion in my old church, I was not saved at the time, and from Matthew 28:19

and Acts 2:41 I could see baptism was only for those who had put their trust in Jesus, so I was baptised again as a believer. I live about 3 kilometres from the Church of God hall, and try my very best to keep the demands of Acts 2:42: *"they devoted themselves to the apostles' teaching and fellowship, the breaking of the bread and the prayers."*

ROLAND WILLIAMS (England)

The Williams family was part of the Church of God in Birkenhead from its inception in 1893 until 2004. As a young lad, aged 10, I attended the Tuesday night class there. I knew full well that I was a sinner and was brought under deep conviction by the message given by Philip Kelly, who used a blackboard lesson with a picture of an egg-timer and 4 short scriptures on that very subject. (1) **T**ime is short (1 Corinthians 7:29). He stressed that there wasn't all the time in the world to turn to Jesus for salvation; (2) **I**t is time to seek the Lord (Hosea 10:12); (3) **M**y times are in Your hands (Psalm 31:15); (4) **E**ternity (Isaiah 57:15) has to be considered. These are all Bible verses that are easy to remember; giving the first letter of each verse to spell out TIME.

I was brought under deep conviction of my sins in my bedroom – the front bedroom at 15 Singleton Avenue. It was my mother who helped me in my troubled state to find peace through believing on the Lord Jesus and what He had done for me, as well as others. It was some time before I was baptised and then brought into the Church of God in Birkenhead, which took place in 1954. My father was deeply concerned that I should recognise that being baptised was something I should take seriously in my pathway of discipleship, largely in Birkenhead, then in Nottingham as a student, and now in Leigh, and that has been an important objective in seeking to bring others to the Saviour. Happily, our children and those whom they have married are in that position, and we trust that others will come to the Saviour as the Spirit of God guides over the years in church and other outreach work.

I hope that all my family and friends will have seriously considered what I have experienced. Then we will meet up in heaven one day, them having taken Jesus as their Saviour and Friend too.

* * *

Epitaph in a graveyard in England:
'I have sinned';
'I have repented';
'I have trusted';
'I have loved';
'I rest';
'I shall rise';
'I shall reign'.

CLOSING APPEAL

DID YOU KNOW?

- Elephants are the only animals that cannot jump!
- Our strongest muscle is our tongue!
- A starfish has no brain.
- It is impossible to sneeze with your eyes open!
- All polar bears are left-handed.
- Butterflies taste with their feet.
- Crocodiles cannot stick out their tongue.
- Mosquitos have teeth.
- 'Cemetery' comes from a Greek word meaning 'dormitory.'

It doesn't really matter if you know these interesting facts - they are not vital to your life. But there is one vital question you need to answer: **'IF YOU DIED TODAY WOULD YOU GO TO HEAVEN OR HELL?'**

"For God so loved the world, that He gave His only begotten Son, that whosoever believes on Him should not perish, but have everlasting life" (John 3:16).

"These things have I written to you, that you may know you have eternal life, even to you that believe on the name of the Son of God" (1 John 5:13).

NOW THAT IS REALLY SOMETHING WORTH KNOWING!

EPILOGUE

I wish to thank all the contributors who responded willingly to my request to send me their 'conversion experience' in writing. This took time, effort, and without doubt, considerable prayer exercise before the Lord. I am truly grateful. A good number have now passed into the presence of the Saviour, awaiting with us, His soon-coming again, when we shall all be forever with the Lord (1 Thessalonians 4:17). I also want to acknowledge the help of Brian Fullarton in the compilation of the material.

Neville